THE INTERNATIONAL CRIMINAL COURT AND THE CRIME OF AGGRESSION

This book has been published with a financial contribution
from the Dipartimento di Scienze Giuridiche dell'Universitá
degli Studi di Trento.

The International Criminal Court and the Crime of Aggression

Edited by

MAURO POLITI and
GIUSEPPE NESI
University of Trento, Italy

ASHGATE

Published by
Ashgate Publishing Limited
Gower House
Croft Road
Aldershot
Hants GU11 3HR
England

Ashgate Publishing Company
Suite 420
101 Cherry Street
Burlington, VT 05401-4405
USA

Ashgate website: http://www.ashgate.com

British Library Cataloguing in Publication Data
The international criminal court and the crime of
    aggression
    1.International Criminal Court - Congresses 2.Aggression
    (International law) - Congresses
    I.Politi, Mauro II.Nesi, Giuseppe
    341.77

Library of Congress Cataloging-in-Publication Data
The International Criminal Court and the crime of aggression / edited by Mauro Politi and
    Giuseppe Nesi.
        p. cm.
    Contains papers delivered at an international meeting held in Trento in May 2001.
    Includes bibliographical references and index.
    ISBN 0-7546-2362-9
        1.Aggression (International law). 2.International Criminal Court. I.Politi, Mauro. II.
    Nesi, Giuseppe.

KZ6374.I58 2004
341.6'2–dc22

2003068876

ISBN 0 7546 2362 9

Printed by TJ International Ltd, Padstow, Cornwall

Contents

The Crime of Aggression and the Relationship between the International Criminal Court and the Security Council

Afterword

**The International Criminal Court and the Crime of Aggression:
From the Preparatory Commission to the Assembly of States
Parties and Beyond**

List of Participants

Ms. Emma BONINO, former Commissioner of the European Union for Humanitarian Affairs

Ms. Mariacarmen COLITTI, No Peace Without Justice, Rome - New York

Professor Luigi CONDORELLI, University of Geneva

Professor Giovanni CONSO, University of Rome

Mrs. Phani DASCALOPOULOU LIVADA, Legal Advisor, Ministry of Foreign Affairs, Athens

Ambassador Nabil ELARABY, International Law Commission, Geneva

Mrs. Paula ESCARAMEIA, Legal Advisor of the Ministry of Foreign Affairs, Lisbon

Ms. Silvia FERNÁNDEZ DE GURMENDI, Ministry of Foreign Affairs, Buenos Aires

Professor Luigi FERRARI BRAVO, Judge of the European Court of Human Rights, Strasbourg

Ms. Socorro FLORES LIERA, Permanent Mission of Mexico to the U.N., Vienna

Professor Giorgio GAJA, University of Florence, Member of the International Law Commission, Geneva

Mr. Mohammed GOMAA, Permanent Mission of Egypt to the U.N., New York

Ms. Victoria HALLUM, Permanent Mission of New Zealand to the U.N., New York

Mr. Hans Peter KAUL, Ministry of Foreign Affairs, Berlin

Professor Umberto LEANZA, University of Rome "Tor Vergata", Head of the Legal Service of the Italian Ministry of Foreign Affairs, Rome

Ms. Marja LEHTO, Ministry of Foreign Affairs, Helsinki

Mrs. Lamia MEKHEMAR, Permanent Mission of Egypt to the U.N., New York

Professor Theodor MERON, New York University, New York, Judge of the International Criminal Tribunal for the former Yugoslavia, The Hague

Professor Giuseppe NESI, University of Trento

Ambassador Enzo PERLOT, President of the University of Trento

Professor Mauro POLITI, University of Trento

Ms. Gaile RAMOUTAR, Permanent Mission of Trinidad and Tobago to the U.N., New York

Professor William A. SCHABAS, National University of Ireland, Galway and Director, Irish Centre for Human Rights

Professor Mohammed Aziz SHUKRI, University of Damascus

Ms. Ioana Gabriela STANCU, Permanent Mission of Romania to the U.N., New York

Professor Tullio TREVES, University of Milan, Judge of the International Tribunal for the Law of the Sea, Hamburg

Ms. Elizabeth WILMSHURST, Legal Service, Foreign and Commonwealth Office, London

Ambassador Juan Antonio YÁÑEZ-BARNUEVO, Ministry of Foreign Affairs, Madrid

Mr. Saeid Mirzaee YENGEJEH, Permanent Mission of the Islamic Republic of Iran to the U.N., New York

Editors' Preface

The Rome Statute of the International Criminal Court entered into force on 1 July 2002 and has been ratified by 90 States. The elections of the judges and prosecutor took place in February and April 2003 and the ICC will soon be fully operational. What was considered not so long ago merely a dream of a few visionaries has become a reality. The challenge is now for the Court to concretely establish its authority as an indispensable institution to fight impunity and contribute to justice and peace in today's world society.

Since the beginning of the ICC process, the University of Trento has been active in promoting scholarly and professional debate on the new Court. In 1999, an international meeting of leading negotiators and eminent scholars was organized in Trento to discuss the main features of the Rome Statute. The papers delivered on that occasion were published in 2001.[1]

Following this path, a second international conference on the ICC was held in Trento from 30 May to 1 June 2001. Diplomats and scholars were invited to address a specific issue that is still unresolved in the post-Rome negotiations: the crime of aggression. Article 5 of the ICC Statute includes aggression, along with genocide, war crimes and crimes against humanity in the list of crimes made subject to the Court's jurisdiction. Yet the Statute postpones the exercise of its jurisdiction over the crime of aggression until such time as further provisions have been prepared on the definition of this crime and on the related conditions for the Court's intervention. After the Rome Conference, the Preparatory Commission for the ICC made considerable efforts towards reaching an agreement, but legal and political difficulties related to issues dealing primarily with the use of force in international relations prevented the Commission from completing its mandate.

The present volume collects the papers given by the participants at the 2001 Trento meeting. In accordance with the program of the meeting, the volume is divided into three parts: the historical background of the crime of aggression; the definition of the crime of aggression, in light of

---

[1] The Proceedings of the 1999 Trento Meeting were published in: Politi and Nesi (eds), *The Rome Statute of the International Criminal Court. A Challenge to Impunity*, Ashgate, Aldershot, 2001.

proposals in the Preparatory Commission; and various points of view on the relationship between the Court's competence in adjudicating cases of alleged crimes of aggression committed by individuals, and the Security Council's competence, under the U.N. Charter, to determine the commission of acts of aggression by a State. The main negotiating documents presented by States and coordinators as well as important studies prepared by the U.N. Secretariat during the Preparatory Commission's work are available at the website: http://www. un.org/law/icc/prepcomm/prepfra.htm or at http://www.jus.unitn.it/icct82/ home.html.

The intent of the Trento initiative was twofold: to clarify the terms of the ongoing debate over the crime of aggression, and to facilitate a better understanding among delegates involved in the negotiating process, which is now set to continue in an *ad hoc* working group open to all member States of the U.N. In both respects, we would like to express our warmest thanks to the speakers and to the other participants for their contribution to the success of the meeting. In particular, we are convinced that the significant progress made on the crime of aggression during the last three sessions of the Preparatory Commission, while not decisive to ensuring a positive outcome, can be seen as evidence of the importance of keeping the dialogue alive on this controversial issue.

Once again, the University of Trento, the Autonomous Province of Trento and the Autonomous Region of Trentino Alto Adige Südtirol were pleased to offer their facilities and financial support to the initiative. To them we are warmly grateful. The colleagues and the personnel from the Law School and the Department of Legal Sciences encouraged us and never stinted on giving advice and useful suggestions as well as concrete contributions to the success of the meeting. The students of the University of Trento and of other Universities showed great enthusiasm and sincere interest in the meeting. Their active participation confirmed once more that they, the students, are the main addressees of such initiatives.

The proceedings of the first Trento meeting were dedicated to the students as future protagonists of international relations. The present volume is dedicated to a person who made an outstanding contribution to both international relations and the University of Trento, the late Ambassador Enzo Perlot, who was an active promoter of the second Trento meeting and presided over its works.

Trento – New York, May 2003

THE CRIME OF AGGRESSION FROM NUREMBERG TO THE ROME STATUTE

1. The Historical Background
UMBERTO LEANZA*

The Nuremberg Military Tribunal: Individual Criminal Responsibility for Crimes Against Peace

In the London Agreement of August 8, 1945, setting up the Military Nuremberg Tribunal, the war of aggression was defined as an international crime, and in particular as a crime against peace. In the Charter of the Tribunal there is no definition for aggression. Only some cases supplementing such a crime are listed as an example, namely:

> planning, preparation, initiation or waging of a war of aggression, or a war in violation of international treaties, agreements or assurances, or participation in a common plan or conspiracy for the accomplishment of any of the foregoing (Art. 6, a.)

The Charter and the decisions issued by the Military Tribunal marked the beginning of a process that had started after World War I. At the same time, it laid the foundations for further developments, in that it sanctioned the final condemnation of aggression, qualifying it as international crime and made the rule prohibiting it imperative.

On 11 December 1946, a few weeks after the conclusion of the Nuremberg trial, the U.N. General Assembly unanimously approved resolution 95 (I), where the international law principles sanctioned by the Charter and by the decisions issued by the military jurisdiction were confirmed and recognized as customary international law principles. The provisions of the London Charter, binding exclusively the twenty-three States Parties to the August 1945 Agreement, thus became the law of an international organization having a universal character, i.e. the United Nations.

---

* University of Rome "Tor Vergata", Head of the Legal Service of the Ministry of Foreign Affairs.

Moreover, the General Assembly charged the newly established Committee on the Codification of International Law with the task of introducing, among its objectives, and as a subject of the utmost importance, the drawing up of a code of crimes against peace and security of mankind. Thus, while during World War II the prohibition to wage aggression wars was not yet codified – in fact, at that time a specific provision on this subject was to be developed – this principle was consolidated by the decisions issued by the Nuremberg and Tokyo Military Tribunals, as well as by the above mentioned General Assembly resolution.

The U.N. Charter and the Prohibition to Threaten and Use Force in International Relations

Although between 1928 and 1942 the conclusion of many treaties of non-aggression would bear witness to a general trend of States to accept the principle to reject war in international relations, only in the United Nations Charter was the principle of the prohibition to use force generally and unequivocally established. Article 2, paragraph 4 of the U.N. Charter is to be considered as the linchpin, the pillar laying the foundations of the current discipline on the use of armed forces in international law. This provision introduced an absolute and unconditioned prohibition both to use and to threaten to use armed forces against territorial integrity or political independence, as well as in any other manner inconsistent with the purposes of the United Nations.

It can be stated that in the present development stage of international law, the prohibition to use force has established itself as a generally recognized customary and binding principle.

The U.N. Charter does not specify in detail the notion of aggression, which was left undefined as a threat to peace and a breach of the peace. During the drafting of the U.N. Charter, many States required it to contain more details on the conditions of applicability of Chapter VII, and more specifically to define aggression or at least to list a certain number of cases justifying the Security Council intervention. The concern was evident that a wide discretionary power of the Security Council to intervene could turn into an arbitrary and unfair use of the monopoly of force by the Security Council permanent members. However, taking into account the lengthy and unfruitful debates on the definition of aggression during the period between the two World Wars, the concern was expressed that the Conference would certainly have come to a standstill if the decision was made to focus on such a thorny question. As a consequence, the decision was made to leave to the U.N. Security Council to appreciate what constitutes a threat to peace, an attack on peace or an act of aggression.

Subsequently, on the occasion of some cases of aggression, where the Security Council was blocked by the cross veto policy, many States required the intervention of the General Assembly to determine the requirements necessary to proclaim an act of aggression. The request to proceed to the definition of this crime was put forward on November 6, 1950, within the First Committee of the General Assembly, when the Soviet Union submitted for the attention of the Committee a draft definition it had already unsuccessfully introduced in 1933.

On November 17, 1950, in its resolution 378/B (V), the General Assembly entrusted the International Law Commission with the mandate of drawing some conclusions on the problem of the definition of aggression. After lengthy debates, the Commission joined the position of its Special Rapporteur, Mr. Spiropolus, stating that a juridical definition of aggression would be an artificial device, which could never be complete enough to include all possible cases of aggression, especially if we consider that aggression methods are constantly developing. In the process of preparation of a draft code of crimes against peace and security of mankind, the Commission therefore decided to introduce among the crimes defined in the draft all acts and threats of aggression, without defining the latter.

Afterwards, in resolution 688 (VII) of December 20, 1952, the General Assembly appointed a Committee composed of fifteen members, entrusted with the task of working out a definition of aggression. At the conclusion of its work, the Committee unanimously decided not to submit the draft to a vote procedure, but rather to convey the proposals to U.N. Member States.

Considering that all previous efforts had not led to a positive result, the General Assembly, in its resolution 859 (IX) of December 4, 1954, established a special Committee composed of nineteen members, entrusted with the task of putting forward a detailed report, followed by a draft definition of aggression. This time too, the Committee admitted that opinions were considerably different and therefore could only refer the question to the General Assembly XI Session.

During that Session, however, the Assembly once again referred the consideration of the report to its Autumn 1957 XII Session, and the resolution adopted on that occasion seemed to express the U.N. intention to "get rid" of the age-old controversy. The General Assembly in fact asked the U.N. Secretary General to invite Member States to express their opinion on this issue and to work out new comments. A new Committee was then charged with the task of examining replies by the States, with a view to establishing the most favorable moment for the Assembly to consider the issue of definition of aggression once again. The Committee, which – due to Western reluctance – could not reach a positive outcome, suspended its work in 1957. The work could hardly progress, bouncing among different committees and sub-committees until 1967, when the Soviet Union re-launched the idea to tackle the issue of the definition of aggression. After an approximately ten year break, the General Assembly, in its resolution 2230 (XXII) of 18 November, 1967, for the third time set up a committee, composed of thirty-five members, chosen according to a geographical distribution criterion. The text approved by the General Assembly in 1974 is the outcome of the work carried out by this Committee.

The Special Committee worked out three different draft definitions. The first definition was prepared by the Soviet Union; the second by Colombia, Cyprus, Ecuador, Ghana, Guyana, Haiti, Madagascar, Mexico, Spain, Uruguay, Uganda and Yugoslavia (the so-called Thirteen-Power Draft); the third draft was prepared by Australia, Canada, Italy, Japan, United States of America and United Kingdom (the so-called Six-Power Draft).

Each draft reflected the particular visions and interests of the drafters. The Soviets, concerned about maintaining control over their satellite territories, introduced the widest possible definition of aggression, together with the overt statement that it would not be possible to proceed to the recognition of sovereignty over those territories that were occupied through the use of force. The Six-Power Draft also reflected the special interest of the States that had worked it out; in particular, the most important point in their definition was the *inherent right to individual or collective self-defense*, which was the main principle invoked by the United States in its "interventions". In spite of all differences, the three drafts substantially agreed on the definition of aggression acts to be included in the resolution.

The General Assembly Resolution 3314 (XXIX) of December 14, 1974 on the Definition of Aggression, with Special Regard to "Indirect Aggression"

On 14 December 1974, the U.N. General Assembly adopted by consensus resolution 3314 (XXIX) on the definition of aggression. A long preamble introduces the ten articles of the Declaration. These provisions do not affect article 39 of the U.N. Charter, nor the Security Council responsibilities. In fact, the Declaration itself recognizes that the Council, considering the circumstances of each individual case, can establish that the commission of one of those acts does not justify its intervention (article 2); that the Council itself can consider as aggression also acts which are not included in the Declaration (article 4); and that, more generally, the definition of aggression contained in the resolution does not affect the functions of the U.N. bodies, as provided for in the Charter (preamble).

Within the framework of the definition of aggression, adopted by the U.N. General Assembly, the provision under art. 3(g) is particularly interesting. It identifies a list of typical aggression acts, which can be qualified as "indirect aggression". The case under article 3(g) identifies two examples of indirect aggression. The first one consists of the sending by a State of armed bands, groups, irregular troops or mercenaries of another State. In this case, the behavior of the State consists of the use of the armed force composed of irregular troops, made up of citizens or mercenaries. These troops differ from the State military corps, in that they do not wear its uniform, or are not formally under the direction or control of a regular staff. Yet, once it is ascertained that these armed bands or irregular groups or mercenaries are sent out by the State, then there is no doubt that their activities, at the international level, can be directly attributed to the State itself. This specific case therefore identifies a particular form of direct aggression, in that the State is responsible for the hostile act, performed by its *de facto* military corps. For these acts to be considered as aggression, they need to be comparable to the direct use of armed forces by a State, in terms of violence employed and damage caused to the State (and in particular to its sovereignty, political independence or territorial integrity).

The second part of the above-mentioned provision deals with a further case, which can be harder to identify. The relevant article makes reference to a *substantial involvement* (*engagement* in the French version) of the State. The seriousness of the acts of force performed by armed bands, groups, irregular troops or mercenaries is common to both cases. However, in the second case, the nature of the activity carried out by the State is different, in that it consists of its *substantial involvement*. Under the subjective viewpoint, participation entails the willful performance of an action or omission, the awareness by the author that he is performing an illicit act, as well as the representation and the will to reach the final event. As to the objective or material aspect of the relation between the activities performed by irregular contingents and the conduct of the State, the *substantial involvement* requires a decisive – albeit not exclusive – *contribution* of the State in the performance of the activities of the armed bands.

In the second case, the behavior of the State is considered: the organization or training of groups, irregular troops, armed bands or mercenaries; the supply of weapons or other war material; the granting of economic or financial aid to one of the parties concerned, with a view to influencing the outcome of the civil war; the making of the State territory available or the State toleration of the use of its own territory as a basis for operational or supply activities, or for the transit of regular or irregular armed forces or war materials.

The so-called indirect aggression was the object of an International Court of Justice decision, which in the 1986 Nicaragua/United States case stated that the provision is part of general international law. According to the Court, the sending by a State of armed bands or groups, irregular troops or mercenaries is to be considered as an armed attack when they perform such serious acts as to be equivalent to a true armed attack performed by regular forces. However, the Court excluded from the notion of armed aggression the mere supply of weapons and logistic support to the insurgents or the rebel forces. Such assistance would only be equivalent to a violation of the principle of non-interference in the domestic affairs of another country and, at the same time, to a *minoris generis* example of the prohibition provided for under article 2, paragraph 4, which does not justify an armed response.

The Crime of Aggression: Criminal Responsibility of the Individual and International Responsibility of States

International crimes of the individual always originate from an action of the State, either because their authors are individuals/State bodies, or because these crimes are the result of policies or choices indirectly favored or otherwise supported by a State. The relevant link clearly appears in the case of aggression.

As a consequence, the commission of international crimes by individuals can actually be accompanied by the simultaneous commission of international crimes by the relevant States. This will automatically be the case not only each time individuals, acting in their capacity as State bodies, will have taken actions the States are directly responsible for, but also each time the latter are to be held liable, in that they have not met their obligations of prevention and repression of merely individual actions. The possible coincidence between criminal responsibility of the individual who is the material author of the action and international liability of the State responsible for that action should not lead to the conclusion that the contents and consequences of the two different responsibilities are to be considered as identical. The opposite is actually true. They are two conceptually different forms of responsibility and the circumstance that they are both provided for by international law should not cause any confusion.

In case of individual criminal responsibility, international law directly intervenes to punish the author of the material conduct. The definition of the specific case is taken from the different domestic criminal laws, whereas the ascertainment of the violation and the punishment modalities are deferred to the State jurisdictional bodies. In such a case, the qualification of a certain behavior as seriously detrimental to the interests of the international community as a whole can be found in general international provisions with which the States are automatically supposed to comply. On the other hand, individual responsibility cannot but be provided for by the States, which are the only ones to enjoy the organizational and binding structure necessary to punish and enforce sentences. In conclusion, the process of enforcement falls within the purview of national criminal systems or else is deferred to international jurisdictional bodies acting on the basis of the will expressed by States in international agreements. Such a will is aimed at setting up a common mechanism which – in an impartial and standard way – can guarantee that crimes are repressed and prevented. Even in a case where the sentence is issued against an individual by an international court, the relevant proceedings are similar to national criminal proceedings, from which they are actually borrowed.

Finally, although in most cases international crimes are committed by a State body, or the State conniving or tolerating the crime is however responsible for them, State responsibility for the action constituting an international crime is not a *sine qua non* condition for the existence of an international crime. The problem lies not so much in establishing whether or not the State can be held liable for the criminal act, but rather in being able to proceed to repression even if, in some cases, the State is to be held accountable.

On the other hand, in the presence of *international responsibility of the State*, the ascertainment of a breach of international rules and its consequences are typical cases provided for by international law. This is also the case of rules designed to meet prevention and repression obligations related to the commission of *crimina juris gentium*. In particular, in order to choose the response to such breaches, it is necessary to analyze general international law provisions dealing with the consequences of the breach. Competence on the issue of violations of State obligation to prevent and repress *crimina juris gentium* is then attributed to the inter-state courts – both arbitration and judicial courts – that have to consider all kinds of disputes between States. On the other hand, this competence is only a "possible" competence. In fact, an international judge – irrespective of the modalities of his appointment – cannot perform his task, unless his jurisdiction is previously accepted by all States parties to a dispute. Moreover, the international jurisdictional function is nowadays still substantially based on arbitration, even if – starting from the end of World War I – some "arrangements" were used (such as the complete compromise clause and the resort to a general arbitration treaty), aimed at obliging States to undergo the judgment of an international court. This allows a contracting State to unilaterally bring another contracting State before an international court invested with the dispute. Moreover, some devices were introduced, aimed at facilitating a wider acceptance of the International Court of Justice. The most significant among them is the so-called "optional clause", according to which

> the States Parties to the Statute of the Court can at any time recognize as compulsory, ipso facto and without special agreement, in relation to any other State accepting the same obligation, the jurisdiction of the Court in all legal disputes (article 36, par. 2, ICJ Statute).

As is well known, the evolution of international practice on individual responsibility for international crimes has always been accompanied by the development of different theories aimed at establishing a special form of State responsibility for the commission of international crimes. They can range from the configuration of the so-called criminal State to the recognition of international criminal responsibility for legal persons, among which States would also be included. During the Nuremberg trial, pivotal significance was attached to the issue whether criminal repression should affect the German State or the individuals who had acted in their capacity as senior officials of the State during the war. The decisions issued by military tribunals also led to the drafting of proposals by private citizens or by the United Nations (e.g. the draft proposal for the establishment of a court on apartheid) which often reflected the idea that an international criminal court should have the authority to judge both natural persons – i.e. persons who materially commit criminal acts – and legal persons, as well as the States on whose behalf or with whose support the individuals act. It could be said that the initial efforts made by the United Nations to establish an International Criminal Court partly failed in that the issue of repression of individual crimes and the issue of international responsibility of States were often the object of useless as well as dangerous confusions.

The parallel drawn by part of the doctrine between the treatment to be applied to serious violations by States and the treatment applied by domestic law to breaches by individuals clashes however with the sharply different structure of the two systems. In fact, criminal law, inspired by the principles of hierarchy and subordination, can hardly be used as a basis for international law, which is governed by the principle of sovereign equality among its members.

International law does not provide for sanctions consisting of punishment. Responses to international crimes do not aim at punishing; in general, they are directed to restore the violated legal order, i.e. to putting a halt to the crime and eliminating its consequences, whenever possible. As a consequence, since criminal responsibility is only there when the rule is accompanied by enforcement measures aimed at repressing the violation, rather than at remedying or terminating it, in the present development stage of international law criminal responsibility of States can hardly be outlined.

The organization of the International Law Commission hinged on codification and progressive development of international rules on responsibility of States on the one hand, and of international rules on the qualification of some individual behavior as *crimina juris gentium* on the other hand. This bears witness to the fact that international criminal responsibility only involves individuals and not States. The difference between these two forms of responsibility clearly emerged from the 1948 Convention on Prevention and Repression of the Crime of Genocide. In Article IV, the said Convention establishes in fact the obligation to extradite or prosecute the author of a crime of genocide, whereas in Article IX it attributes to the International Court of Justice the responsibility of settling disputes between Contracting Parties on the interpretation, implementation or enforcement of the Convention, including disputes related to responsibility of States on the issue of genocide.

This distinction is also reiterated in the Statute of the International Criminal Court. It is true that, during the preparatory work, some proposals were put forward aimed at introducing criminal responsibility for international crimes not only in relation to natural persons, but also to legal persons, but the relevant proposals were not included in the Rome Statute. However, in order to rule out criminal responsibility of the State, these proposals always excluded the possibility of listing States among legal bodies. Article 25, para. 4, of the Statute of the Court, unequivocally reads that *no provision in this Statute relating to individual criminal responsibility shall affect the responsibility of States under international law.* This wording was the object of no negative comments whatsoever, and was widely accepted during the preparatory work and by the Conference itself.

Hence, if an international court were eventually called to judge a State, it would only deal with State responsibility, and not with individual criminal responsibility. By the same token, the International Criminal Court will exert its jurisdiction exclusively on individuals, and only individuals/State bodies will therefore be submitted to judgment.

The Crime of Aggression in the Draft Statute of the International Criminal Court Submitted to the Rome Conference: Relations Between the ICC and the UN Security Council

With reference to the ICC, the problem of a possible overlapping of responsibilities (criminal responsibility of individuals and international responsibility of States) clearly emerges in the Rome Statute.

If compared to other crimes listed in the Statute, in the case of aggression the distinction between crime of the State and crime of the individual is particularly blurred. In this sense, aggression can be considered as a strongly "politicized" crime, in that the criminal responsibility of the individual/body necessarily depends on the existence of an act of aggression of the State of which the individual is a citizen.

As already known, *like-minded* States have always reiterated their support to the introduction of the crime of aggression among those falling within the responsibilities of the Court. They were convinced that its exclusion would constitute a step backward *vis-à-vis* the Charter of the Nuremberg Tribunal, which included such a crime.

These arguments were opposed by those Countries which feared that their political and military leaders could face prosecution for an act of aggression. They put forward two arguments: the inclusion of aggression could lead to a "politicization" of the recourse to the Court, and encourage unjustified reports aimed at propaganda. Moreover, they purported that international law did not provide for a universally accepted definition of aggression, useful above all to ascertain criminal responsibility of individuals.

The draft Statute submitted to the Rome Conference widely reflected the difficulties inherent in the definition of the crime of aggression.

While agreeing on the fact that the crime of aggression can exclusively cover acts committed by individuals controlling or directing a political or military action of the aggressing State (as established also by the Nuremberg Tribunal), the States attending the Rome Conference had different opinions on the notion of the crime to be agreed upon. In particular, the Draft Statute submitted to the Rome Conference included the following three options:

The first option envisaged a general definition and did not contain a detailed list of the elements of crime. In this case, the ICC would be entitled to decide which acts would be relevant in each individual case. The Court could therefore be exposed to the criticism of inconsistency with the principle of legality (*nullum crimen sine lege*).

The second option, supported by a considerable number of Arab and African States, included both a general definition and a list of acts considered as elements of the crime of aggression. Such a list was taken from the 1974 declaration of the U.N. General Assembly. Resolution 3314, however, is not part of general international law and refers to the definition of international responsibility of States. Its wording could therefore be used as a guide by the U.N. Security Council, but could not provide the Court's judges with a definition of the conduct to be punished and hence could not be used to assess possible criminal responsibilities of the individual/body.

The third option, put forward by Germany, aimed at reconciling the two previously mentioned options. It established that an armed attack by a State against the territorial integrity or the political independence of another State was to specifically have the objective to attain or result into a military occupation, or an annexation of the aggressed State. Such a solution, however, could be criticized as being unjustifiably restrictive, in that it excluded other similarly serious actions which, however, were not aimed at occupying or annexing the territory of another State (such as an attack to an aircraft or a ship).

This was the reason why the negotiations resulted in a standstill. Moreover, the situation is aggravated by another sensitive issue: the role of the Security Council in the process of ascertaining the commission of an act of aggression.

The problem concerned relations between the Security Council and the future ICC, which should safeguard on the one hand the political role of the Security Council in maintaining international peace and security, and on the other hand the characteristics of independence and impartiality typical of a jurisdictional body.

According to the permanent members of the Security Council, the competence of the ICC over the individual crime of aggression had to be subjected to the ascertainment carried out by the Security Council of the presence of an act of aggression by the State.

On the other hand, most Arab and developing countries held the opinion that the Court had to act fully independently, both with regard to the ascertainment of the presence of an act of aggression by a State and with regard to its consequences in the field of individual responsibilities.

Actually, it seemed that there were no legal or practical reasons justifying a substantial subordination of the jurisdictional function of the ICC to the competence of the Security Council in the field of maintenance of international peace and security. In fact, they are objectively different responsibilities, pertaining to distinct law cases: the former can be exerted vis-à-vis the individual, while the latter aims at eliminating situations or a State conduct detrimental to international peace and security. Moreover, such a subordination is not envisaged in the case of the International Court of Justice, which is indeed called to exert its jurisdiction over States and whose act could interfere with the measures that the Security Council can adopt under Chapter VII of the U.N. Charter.

During the Rome Conference, a proposal was put forward to consider the necessary Security Council decision on the presence of an act of aggression like a mere *condition for prosecution vis-à-vis* the jurisdiction of the Court. The Court could hence re-consider the presence of aggression in a given conduct, as well as the individual responsibility of its authors.

A further proposal tabled by Cameroon during the Rome Conference envisaged that, when the crime of aggression is submitted to the ICC, the ICC would be obliged to submit the question to the Security Council for a declaration on the existence of aggression. Should the Council fail to make a decision in a reasonable time, the ICC could initiate its proceedings.

However, the proposal was not discussed in detail. And indeed, the relations between the Security Council and the ICC on the subject of the crime of aggression were not exhaustively dealt with during the Rome Conference, not only because of the short time granted to negotiators, but above all because of the absence of a solution on its definition.

Aggression was therefore one of the most difficult questions the Conference had to face. Actually, until the last moment the very introduction of the crime of aggression among the responsibilities of the Court was uncertain.

A wide majority of States participating in the Rome Conference decided that aggression would be part of the crimes falling within the jurisdiction of the ICC. However, in the absence of a wording covering both the definition of the crime of aggression and the relations between the future Criminal Court and the Security Council, Article 5, paragraph 2, of the Statute only envisages that the Court can deal with an individual crime of aggression after the relevant notion is defined in an *ad hoc* provision, to be adopted according to the normal procedures provided for with regard to amendments to the Statute. Such a provision should also regulate conditions for the exercise of the jurisdiction of the Court on this subject and should be consistent with the relevant provisions of the UN Charter.

The wording accepted in Article 5, paragraph 2 of the Statute can therefore be considered as an expedient aimed at overcoming the temporary standstill of the preparatory work, with a view to avoiding an excessive delay in the entry into force of the Statute.

2. Origins of the Criminalization of Aggression: How Crimes Against Peace Became the "Supreme International Crime"

WILLIAM A. SCHABAS[*]

In October 1943, the Allies launched the United Nations War Crimes Commission. As the name of the Commission suggested, the remit was to prepare the prosecution of "war crimes". Although reasonable people might then have disagreed about the content of what constituted violations of the laws and customs of war, the concept – *jus in bello* – had been well-known to jurists, especially international lawyers, since ancient times, as we can see from such diverse sources as the works of Shakespeare, Homer and Grotius. But as the deliberations progressed, during 1944, the expert members of the Commission began to explore the possibility of including the waging of aggressive war within the subject-matter jurisdiction of their work on war crimes. But, at least at the outset, the American and British governments were opposed to prosecution for the waging of aggressive war, and the Commission was divided on the subject. In December 1944, it decided that it would not take a position on this difficult subject.

Six months later, opinions had evolved. The London Conference authorised the great trial of the Nazi leadership at Nuremberg on the basis of both war crimes and crimes against peace, as well as crimes against humanity. On 30 September – 1 October, the final judgment of the International Military Tribunal, discussing the nature of crimes against peace, said that "[t]o initiate a war of aggression, therefore, is not only an international crime; it is the supreme international crime differing only

---

[*] Professor of Human Rights Law, National University of Ireland, Galway, and Director of the Irish Centre for Human Rights.

from other war crimes in that it contains within itself the accumulated evil of the whole".[1] In other words, acts that international criminal law experts, in December 1944, could not even agree were punishable, had reached the apex of the pyramid of wrongdoing.

The *Rome Statute of the International Criminal Court* includes "aggression" – a more contemporary formulation of the term "crimes against peace" – within the subject matter jurisdiction of the new Court, but then makes prosecution subject to adoption of a definition and upon agreement on the conditions under which it shall exercise jurisdiction with respect to the crime. Debate about these issues began only slowly after the 1998 Rome Conference, but appears now to be taken in greater earnest. The debates, both at Rome and since then, bear more than a passing resemblance to the disputes in 1944 and 1945.

The process and the issues involved in prosecution of aggression by the International Criminal Court are the subject of other papers in this volume, and will not be discussed here. But by way of introduction, it seems useful to recall that aggression is very much of an enigmatic crime that does not fit easily within the scheme of the International Criminal Court. For example, the complementarity regime, which is very much the gatekeeper to prosecution, seems virtually inapplicable, given that practically no States have national criminal legislation governing aggression, nor can it generally be subsumed – unlike genocide, crimes against humanity and war crimes – within the framework of ordinary offences that are found in all criminal codes, such as murder, rape and so on. As things stand today, practically every State party to the *Rome Statute* is either "unwilling or unable genuinely" to carry out investigation or prosecution of the crime of aggression.[2]

Nor is there any serious suggestion in the literature, or in the case law, that aggression is the type of crime for which universal jurisdiction may be exercised. Here again, the absence of national legislation makes the question highly academic in any event. There is certainly no practice to indicate a customary norm. The idea does not appear to have even crossed the mind of the judges of the International Court of Justice who examined the matter in the recent *Arrest Warrant* case.[3] Professor Alain Pellet, speaking in the International Law Commission in 1995, spoke of the

---

[1]   *United States of America et al.* v. *Goering* et al., International Military Tribunal, Judgment, 30 September-1 October 1946, (1947) 41 *Am J. Int'l L.* 172, at p. 186.

[2]   *Rome Statute of the International Criminal Court*, U.N. Doc. A/CONF.183/9, art. 17(1)(a)

[3]   *Arrest Warrant of 11 April 2000 (Democratic Republic of the Congo* v. *Belgium)*, Judgment, 15 February 2002. See especially: Joint separate opinion of Judges Higgins, Kooijmans and Buergenthal; Dissenting opinion of Judge Van Den Wyngaert.

absurdity of the Municipal Court of Benghazi ruling that Luxembourg had committed aggression in Mali.[4]

It should seem obvious enough that ongoing work aimed at plugging the hole in the *Rome Statute* is to a large extent an exercise in the progressive development of international law, rather than in its codification, one of *lex ferenda* rather than *lex lata*. And so it was, it would seem, in London in 1944 and 1945. Perhaps the lessons from that effort will be helpful in assisting those who are now wrestling with these difficult issues. In particular, this paper will attempt to understand how crimes against peace, which in 1943 had barely figured on the prosecutorial agenda, became transformed in less than two years into the "supreme international crime".

Background to the Debate: Prosecutions after the First World War

Aside from a few obscure examples that are little more than historical curiosities,[5] the real story of international criminal prosecution begins with the First World War. It is well known that the *Treaty of Versailles* contemplated, in articles 228 to 230, the prosecution before Allied military tribunals of German combatants charged with "violation of the laws and customs of war".[6] The two sides quarrelled about the list of suspects and the forum of prosecution, but the principle under which a German soldier who commanded a U-boat or a prisoner-of-war camp could be held liable for killing shipwrecked survivors or abusing prisoners was uncontroversial. We need only recall the finely-honed vision of legal obligation manifested by Erich von Stroheim in the Jean Renoir film classic *La grande illusion* to confirm the currency of the notion of "laws and customs of war". Although much was unsatisfactory about the overall record of prosecution, it cannot be said that the Supreme Court of the Empire, in the trials held pursuant to articles 228 *et seq.*, had any great difficulty with defence arguments of *nullum crimen sine lege.*

---

[4]   U.N. Doc. A/CN.4/SER.A/1995, p. 36.
[5]   Georg Schwarzenberger, "The Judgment of Nuremberg", (1947) 21 *Tulane L. Rev.* 329, pp. 329-330.
[6]   James F. Willis, *Prologue to Nuremberg: The Politics and Diplomacy of Punishing War Criminals of the First World War*, Westport, Connecticut: Greenwood Press, 1982; Sheldon Glueck, *War Criminals. Their Prosecution and Punishment*, New York: Knopf, 1944.

The idea that the waging of aggressive war, or "crimes against peace", or something resembling it, might be prosecuted appears to have originated with the British. Lord Curzon launched the debate at a meeting of the Imperial War Cabinet on 30 November 1918.[7] The British emphasized trying the Kaiser and other leading Germans. At the time, they showed little or no inclination towards accountability for the persecution of innocent minorities such as the Armenians in Turkey.[8] The objective was to punish "those who were responsible for the War or for atrocious offences against the laws of war".[9] As Lloyd George explained, "[t]here was also a growing feeling that war itself was a crime against humanity..."[10]

The Inter-Allied Commission on the Responsibility of the Authors of War (known as the Commission on Responsibilities), that was established at the Paris Peace Conference in early 1919, recommended that the crime of waging aggressive war should not be prosecuted:

> The premeditation of a war of aggression dissimulated under a peaceful pretence, then suddenly declared under false pretexts, is conduct which the public conscience reproves and which history will condemn, but b y reason of the purely optional character of the Institutions at The Hague for the maintenance of peace (International Commission of Inquiry, Mediation and Arbitration) a war of aggression may not be considered as an act directly contrary to positive law, or one which can be successfully brought before a tribunal such as the Commission is authorised to consider under its Terms of Reference... We therefore do not advise that the acts which provoked the war should be charted against their authors and made the subject of proceedings before a tribunal.[11]

But the Commission also recommended that "[i]t is desirable that for the future *penal sanctions* should be provided for such grave outrages against the elementary principles of international law."[12]

---

[7] David Lloyd George, *The Truth About the Peace Treaties*, Vol. I, London: Victor Gollancz, 1938, pp. 93-114. For a discussion of the project, see: "Question of International Criminal Jurisdiction", U.N. Doc. A/CN.4/15, paras. 6-13; Howard S. Levie, *Terrorism in War, The Law of War Crimes*, New York: Oceana, 1992, pp. 18-36; "First report on the draft Code of Offences against the Peace and Security of Mankind, by Mr. Doudou Thiam, Special Rapporteur", U.N. Doc. A/CN.4/364, paras. 7-23.

[8] David Lloyd George, *ibid.*, pp. 93-114.

[9] *Ibid.*, p. 93.

[10] *Ibid.*, p. 96.

[11] United Nations War Crimes Commission, *History of the United Nations War Crimes Commission and the Development of the Laws of War*, London: His Majesty's Stationery Office, 1948, p. 237.

[12] *Ibid.*, p. 238 (emphasis in the original).

These words were not really heeded, and the Peace Conference adopted article 227 of the *Treaty of Versailles*: "The Allied and Associated Powers publicly arraign William II of Hohenzollern, formerly German Emperor, for a supreme offence against international morality and the sanctity of treaties." The provision hardly belongs in the instrument at all, as it does not establish rights and obligations of the States parties. It is purely declaratory. In an answer to German protests about article 227, the Allies readily conceded that this indictment "has not a juridical character as regards its substance, but only in its form. The ex-Emperor is arraigned as a matter of high international policy..."[13]

Kaiser Wilhelm was never brought to trial, but had the proceedings ever taken place, his defence counsel would surely have made much of how the concept of a "a supreme offence against international morality and the sanctity of treaties" could not be reconciled with the principle of legality. It is hard to find a better example of a legal norm that deserves the epithet "void for vagueness" than article 227 of the *Treaty of Versailles*. And of course unlike both war crimes and crimes against humanity, which were underpinned by ordinary crimes defined in the national criminal law of all countries, prosecution for this "supreme offence" was truly unprecedented. The Kaiser escaped arrest by fleeing to The Netherlands, which was neutral and was not a party to the peace negotiations. When Georges Clemenceau, acting on behalf of the victorious powers, requested the surrender of the German Emperor, the Dutch answered: "L'offense supreme contre la morale internationale et l'autorité des traités ... ne figure pas dans les nomenclatures des infractions pénales inserées dans les lois de Hollande ou les traités par elle conclus."[14]

Article 227 of the *Treaty of Versailles* did not use the term "aggression" or "crimes against peace" because at the time these were not considered to be acts contrary to international law,[15] let alone subject to individual prosecution. But to the extent that the provision was targeted at military and civilian leaders for the waging of a war illegally – that is, in violation of treaties of peace or non-aggression – we find the antecedents of article VI(a) of the Charter of the International Military Tribunal. During

---

[13] *Reply of the Allied and Associated Powers to the Observations of the German Delegation and the Conditions of Peace*, Paris, 16 June 1919, HMSO, Misc. No. 4 (1919).
[14] (1920) 8 *Revue de droit international* 40.
[15] See, on this point: Quincy Wright, "Changes in the Conception of War", (1924) *18 Am. J. Int'l L.* 755; Quincy Wright, "The Concept of Aggression in International Law", (1935) 29 *Am. J. Int'l L.* 373.

the inter-war years, much progress was made in the prohibition of aggressive war, the benchmark being the Kellogg-Briand Pact of 1928. Yet even when war broke out anew in 1939, it was hard to argue that the law had changed significantly over twenty years, and certainly not with respect to individual criminal responsibility.

Work of the United Nations War Crimes Commission

The United Nations War Crimes Commission was established at a Diplomatic Conference convened at the Foreign Office in London on 20 October 1943. Most of the Allies participated actively in its activities, with the notable and important exception of the Soviet Union. The Commission undertook preparatory investigative work for future prosecutions as well as preparation of their legal aspects. At one point, the Commission actually drafted the statute of a future international criminal court.[16] The Commission was to a large extent superseded in mid-1945, when the initiative for international criminal prosecution was taken up by the four powers at the London Conference.

According to the official history of the United Nations War Crimes Commission, "[b]y far the most important issue of substantive law to be studied by the Commission and its Legal Committee was the question of whether aggressive war amounts to a criminal act".[17] Whether or not "aggression" might fit within the overall mandate of the Commission appears have been raised for the first time in March 1944 during the first sessions of the Legal Committee, by Bohuslav Ecer of Czechoslovakia. He considered that "the paramount crime of the Axis powers" was the "launching and waging of the war... Their aims [were] to enslave foreign nations, to destroy the civilisation of those nations, and physically to annihilate a considerable section of their populations on racial, political or religious grounds".[18]

Ecer, a barrister who was also deputy mayor of Brno, had been arguing this position since as early as October 1942, during sessions of the London International Assembly. The Assembly was an unofficial body that had been established at the initiative of Viscount Cecil of Chelwood under the *aegis* of the League of Nations Union. Its members were designated by Allied Governments. In 1942 it decided to establish a commission to study

---

[16] United Nations War Crimes Commission, *supra* note 11, pp. 107-118.

[17] *Ibid.*, p. 180.

[18] Arieh J. Kochavi, *Prelude to Nuremberg, Allied War Crimes Policy and the Question of Punishment*, Chapel Hill and London: University of North Carolina Press, 1998, p. 97.

the question of war crimes. This commission agreed to a broad definition of war crimes that encompassed the waging of aggressive war.

Responding to a declaration to the media by the American statesman Sumner Welles, which indicated that the future international war crimes commission would deal with those responsible for "war atrocities" but that it was still a question "whether Hitler will be one", Ecer wrote,

> This declaration arouses the impression that certain politicians in the United States of America do not regard the launching of a war of aggression, nor hence, a war of aggression in itself, as a crime, but only the "atrocities" committed in the course of the war, and that the penal responsibility of Hitler, not only for the war, but even for "war atrocities" is doubtful. We must dispose of this confused thinking and remove all doubts.[19]

Ecer argued that since the First World War, the law on the waging of aggressive war had been transformed, principally as a result of the Kellogg-Briand Pact, and that it was now correct to state that "[a]ggressive warfare, in itself, even if waged without 'atrocities' and in full compliance with the conventions of The Hague and Geneva, is a crime".

Ecer insisted that with respect to "war atrocities", no international tribunal was really necessary, as these could be prosecuted under existing law by the States upon whose territories they had been committed. But for the crime of aggressive war, it would be necessary to set up "a high international tribunal composed of judges representing all the countries at war with Germany, and to this tribunal all the countries concerned will assign their penal jurisdiction for this special case".[20] Ecer prepared a proposal for the London International Assembly that said:

> Aggressive war is a crime, and by its character an international crime, because it aims against peace and international order. The total aggressive war started by Germany and her allies in 1939 is additionally an international crime in its territorial extent and the number of victims of the aggression.
>
> Not only the aggressor States as such, but also their rulers and military leaders are personally responsible in the eyes of the law for the gigantic chain of crimes which compose this war and which are punishable under the criminal laws of the countries affected.

---

[19] Bohuslav Ecer, "The Punishment of War Criminals", confidential document dated 10 October 1942 submitted to the London International Assembly, Commission II on the Trial of War Criminals, reprinted in George J. Lankevich, ed., *Archives of the Holocaust, Vol. 16*, New York and London: Garland, 1990, pp. 1-4.

[20] *Ibid.*

The penalty according to all these laws is death.[21]

Ecer's proposal to include aggressive war within the overall scope of war crimes was favourably received by the Legal Committee of the United Nations War Crimes Commission when it met in March 1944. The concept was included in its draft resolution on the "Scope of the Retributive Action of the United Nations", where it was defined as "[t]he crimes committed for the purpose of preparing or launching the war, irrespective of the territory where these crimes have been committed". But its submission to the Plenary Commission in June 1944 was returned to the Legal Committee for further study. Opponents were apparently concerned that the proposal would be too radical for member governments.[22]

A subcommittee of the Legal Committee was established to pursue work on this subject. The British expert Arnold McNair advised the subcommittee on the issue, taking the view that aggressive war, though reprehensible, did not constitute a crime under international law.[23] McNair argued that the State itself could not be the subject of criminal liability, and that consequently aggressive war could not be considered a crime on an individual level.[24] His views reflected the current position of the British government. A majority of the Legal Committee accepted McNair's opinion, and said so in its report: "[A]cts committed by individuals merely for the purpose of preparing for and launching aggressive war, are, lege lata, not 'war crimes'."[25] Bohuslav Ecer issued a minority report in which he contended that by focusing on the criminal nature of the plan for aggressive war, other related crimes like the extermination of racial groups would then be judged not as war crimes but as part of a criminal war.[26]

The sub-committee's two reports were considered by the plenary War Crimes Commission in October 1944. Members were quite divided on which of the reports, majority or minority, to adopt. It was agreed to postpone any decision in order to permit consultations with governments.

---

[21]   United Nations War Crimes Commission, *supra* note 11, pp. 100-101.

[22]   Arieh J. Kochavi, *supra* note 18, p. 97; United Nations War Crimes Commission, *supra* note 11, pp. 180-181.

[23]   Arieh J. Kochavi, *supra* note 18, pp. 97-98; United Nations War Crimes Commission, *supra* note 11, p. 140.

[24]   United Nations War Crimes Commission, *supra* note 11, p. 181.

[25]   "Report of the Sub-Committee appointed to consider whether the preparation and launching of the present war should be considered 'war crimes'", Doc. C.55, 27 September 1944.

[26]   "Minority Report presented by Dr. B. Ecer on the question whether the preparation and launching of the present war should be considered as crimes being within the scope of the United Nations War Crimes Commission", Doc. C56, 27 September 1944.

Sir Cecil Hurst, who chaired the Commission, reported to Sir Anthony Eden of the British government that this had become an issue in the Commission because of fears that those responsible for the war would go unpunished.[27] The Foreign Office replied to Hurst expressing its view that aggressive war *per se* was not a war crime. He then circulated a memo to the Commission recommending that no vote be taken on the issue, and his advice was followed. Hurst said he was concerned that the debate could be misinterpreted by public opinion, and that opposition to the concept of prosecution for waging aggressive war might be construed as a general rejection of the criminality of the Nazi leaders, which it was not.[28]

Within the United States government, the debate about whether aggressive war should be punishable only surfaced in November 1944. As Bradley Smith's study demonstrates, the possibility of prosecution for "aggressive war" bitterly divided American officials and policy-makers. A memorandum prepared by Colonel William C. Chanler, a War Department official and protégé of Secretary of War Henry Stimson, argued that the Kellogg-Briand Pact of 1928 had operated a major change in the applicable law.[29] Chanler toyed with the idea that although those who waged war in breach of the Pact might not incur individual criminal liability, they lost the legal protections available to "lawful belligerents" (a concept to which Pentagon lawyers seem very attached, even today). This meant "any person or group of persons who engage in such a course of conduct as that followed by the Nazis in connection with the present war are violators of the Pact and as such are common criminals".[30]

A somewhat more ingenious strategy was being devised by Murray Bernays, who sought to fold everything under the rubric of "conspiracy". As he explained, lawful acts might nevertheless be steps in a conspiracy, although they would not necessarily be war crimes. Bernays explained that violating the Kellogg-Briand Pact might not in itself be a crime, but it could be considered conspiratorial and thereby "lend support to the theory of group criminality".[31]

But Stimson's instructions to Herbert Pell, who represented the United States at the United Nations War Crimes Commission, were similar

---

[27] Arieh J. Kochavi, *supra* note 18, p. 99.

[28] "Examination of the question whether the preparation and launching of the present war can be considered a 'war crime'", Doc. C.64, 20 November 1944; Arieh J. Kochavi, *supra* note 18, p. 100; United Nations War Crimes Commission, *supra* note 11, 184.

[29] Bradley F. Smith, *The Road to Nuremberg*, New York: Basic Books, 1990, p. 95.

[30] *Ibid.*, p. 97.

[31] Arieh J. Kochavi, *supra* note 18, p. 207.

to those of the British Foreign Office. Australia, India and Greece directed their representatives to oppose taking any decision on whether or not to include aggressive war within the scope of war crimes, and other delegates indicated that they had not yet received any instructions.[32] New Zealand and Yugoslavia favoured the prosecution of aggressive war, and Australia subsequently adopted a similar position as well.[33] But in the result, the United Nations War Crimes Commission did not resolve the question, at least, not until after the London Conference of the four powers – the United States of America, the United Kingdom, France and the Soviet Union – had decided that "crimes against peace" should be part of the subject-matter jurisdiction of the International Military Tribunal.

Before moving on to the London Conference, however, it is important to consider briefly the context in which these discussions were taking place. There was considerable public concern that the leading Nazis would go unpunished. The Soviet Union was particularly preoccupied by the possibility that its Western Allies might ultimately back down from prosecution, and more specifically prosecution of the Nazi leaders.[34] The idea had been nourished by statements like those of Sumner Welles, referred to above, that hinted at accountability for the subalterns and impunity for their commanders. After all, that had been the pattern at the only real precedent for such action, the Leipzig trials that followed the First World War.

The debate was also being influenced by the establishment of the United Nations organization itself. The Dumbarton Oaks Proposals, adopted in 1944, pledged United Nations members to refrain from the threat or use of force. The provision in question is the antecedent of article 2(4) of the Charter of the United Nations. Inspired by this development, in early 1945 members of the United Nations War Crimes Commission sought to make representations to the San Francisco Conference on the subject of punishment for the preparation of aggressive war. The Commission's Enforcement Committee recommended the following norm: "Any person in the service of any State who has violated any rule of international law forbidding the threat or use of force, or any rule concerning warfare, especially the obligation to respect the generally recognized principles of humanity, shall be held individually responsible for these acts, and may be brought to trial and punishment before the civil or military tribunals of any State which may secure custody of his person."[35] This met with general

---

[32]   United Nations War Crimes Commission, *supra* note 11, p. 184.
[33]   *Ibid.*, pp. 184-185.
[34]   Arieh J. Kochavi, *supra* note 18, p. 229.
[35]   United Nations War Crimes Commission, *supra* note 11, p. 186.

agreement, but the Commission was split on a companion proposal aimed at giving the principle a retroactive effect, so as to apply to Nazi war criminals as well as future aggressors.[36] Ultimately, the *Charter of the United Nations* was silent on the issue of individual criminal liability, nor can it be interpreted as taking any position on the conduct of aggressive war in the past.

The London Conference

In June 1945, representatives from France, the Soviet Union, the United States and the United Kingdom convened in London in order to prepare the groundwork for trial of the Nazi leaders. The discussions built upon the work of the United Nations War Crimes Commission.[37] Their work concluded on 8 August 1945 with the adoption of the London Agreement, to which is annexed the *Charter of the International Military Tribunal* which would soon convene in Nuremberg.[38]

The documentation on the debates within the Government of the United States is the most extensive, and any analysis of the drafting of the Charter of the Nuremberg Tribunal inexorably focuses on this material. By May 1945, the United States Department of Justice was already making detailed preparations of the case against the Nazi leaders. Justice Robert Jackson's staff pushed for a prosecutorial strategy built around the claim that prior to 1 September 1939, the Nazi leaders had "entered into a common plan or enterprise" to establish "complete German domination of Europe and eventually the world".[39] Aggressive war conspiracy was to become, noted Bradley Smith, "the transcendent theme of Nazism".[40]

In his 6 June 1945 report to President Truman, Justice Jackson set out his proposal to make war of aggression a crime.[41] In preparation for the London Conference, Jackson's proposal to include aggressive war within the subject-matter jurisdiction of the Tribunal was submitted to the other

---

[36] *Ibid.*

[37] For discussion of relations between the two bodies, see United Nations War Crimes Commission, *supra* note 11, pp. 456-457.

[38] *Agreement for the Prosecution and Punishment of Major War Criminals of the European Axis, and Establishing the Charter of the International Military Tribunal (I.M.T.)*, annex, (1951) 82 UNTS 279.

[39] Bradley F. Smith, *supra* note 29, p. 233.

[40] *Ibid.*

[41] "Report to the President by Mr. Justice Jackson, June 6, 1945", in *Report of Robert H. Jackson, United States Representative to the International Conference on Military Trials*, Washington: U.S. Government Printing Office, 1949, pp. 42-54..

three powers on 14 June 1945, and then formally presented on 26 June to the London Conference. It was the same day as the San Francisco Conference was outlawing the use of force in the *Charter of the United Nations*, as Ben Ferencz has pointed out.[42] The American proposal included "Launching a war of aggression" among the crimes that would be punishable.[43] A United Kingdom submission issued a few days later concurred on this point.[44] Soviet enthusiasm for the prosecution of aggression had never really been in doubt, and the international law arguments in support had been developed by its leading specialist Professor A.N. Trainin.

The issue was discussed at length on 19 July. The French delegate André Gros questioned whether the four-power conference could legitimately make new law on the subject, and expressed the view that France did not consider the waging of aggressive war to be a crime that incurred individual liability.[45] The delegates considered whether or not aggression should be defined, but leaned towards referring only to applicable international agreements that might have been violated by Germany. Accordingly, the British Delegation submitted a proposal that listed the following crime: "Domination over other nations or aggression against them in the manner condemned or foresworn in (*inter alia*) the following Pacts or Declarations…".[46]

By 31 July the United States had reformulated the provision as "The Crime of War".[47] It included a specific reference to the Kellogg-Briand Pact. At the 2 August session,[48] Britain pointed out that the Soviet specialist, Professor Trainin, had treated aggression not as a "crime of war" but a "crime against peace", and agreement was quickly reached on this minor change in terminology. In the final version, adopted 8 August, "crime" became "crimes", presumably for the sake of parallelism with "crimes against humanity", and the specific mention of the Kellogg-Briand

---

[42] Benjamin B. Ferencz, "Defining Aggression: Where it Stands and Where it's Going", (1972) 66 *Am. J. Int'l L.* 491, at p. 492.

[43] "Revision of American Draft of Proposed Agreement, June 14, 1945", in *Report of Robert H. Jackson, United States Representative to the International Conference on Military Trials, supra* note 41, pp. 55-60.

[44] *Ibid.*, p. 87.

[45] Jackson, "Minutes of Conference Session of July 19, 1945", pp. 295-296, also 297.

[46] "Proposed Revision of Definition of 'Crimes' (Article 6), Submitted by British Delegation, July 20, 1945", p. 312.

[47] "Revision of Definition of 'Crimes' Submitted by American Delegation, July 31, 1945", p. 395.

[48] "Minutes of Conference Session of August 2, 1945", pp. 416-417.

Pact was removed in favour of a general reference to "international treaties, agreements or assurances".

The "supreme international crime" expression used by the Nuremberg judges to describe crimes against peace was an almost inexorable consequence of the prosecutorial strategy and the evidence that was led before the Tribunal. In his opening statement, Jackson said "This inquest represents the practical effort of four of the most mighty of nations, with the support of fifteen more, to utilise International law to meet the greatest menace of our times – aggressive war". The judges did not invent the focus on aggressive war, they were pointed in that direction by Jackson, by the London Conference and by politics.

Comments and Conclusions

This brief historical overview is an attempt to understand what brought the International Military Tribunal, in its final judgment, to describe crimes against peace as the "supreme international crime". The concept had been largely rejected at Versailles, where it was recognized that the indictment of the Kaiser was more about "high international policy" than it was about criminal law and individual accountability. Nevertheless, much happened to change the position taken by international law towards wars of aggression in the years between 1919 and 1939, and these developments were consolidated in the prohibition of the threat or the use of force in article 2(4) of the *Charter of the United Nations*.

In an interview some years ago, the Dutch judge at the Tokyo Trial, R.V.A. Röling, told Professor Antonio Cassese: "[I]n my view, aggressive war was not a crime under international law at the beginning of the war."[49] This issue was at the heart of the debates within the United Nations War Crimes Commission, a relatively representative body that included delegates not only from the major powers but from smaller countries as well. There was genuine division on the subject, reflecting a general uncertainty not only about whether or not aggressive war belonged within the remit of the Commission but also whether prosecution might breach the principle *nullum crimen sine lege*.

In its final judgment, the Nuremberg Tribunal essentially conceded the fact that punishing crimes against peace amounted to retroactive prosecution. It appeared to view prosecution for aggressive war as a

---

[49] B.V.A. Röling and Antonio Cassese, *The Tokyo Trial and Beyond*, London: Polity Press, 1993, p. 98.

legitimate exception to the general rule: "To assert that it is unjust to punish those who in defiance of treaties and assurances have attacked neighboring states without warning is obviously untrue, for in such circumstances the attacker must know that he is doing wrong, and so far from it being unjust to punish him, it would be unjust if his wrong were allowed to go unpunished." At the time, *nullum crimen* does not seem to have had the sacred, non-derogable status that it would come to take on.[50]

But when the judges at Nuremberg, and at Tokyo came to punish persons who had been convicted of the "supreme crime", they hesitated.[51] Nobody found guilty of crimes against peace and not of the other two categories, war crimes against crimes against humanity, was sentenced to death. For example, Rudolph Hess was convicted of crimes against peace and acquitted of war crimes and crimes against humanity. He received a sentence of life imprisonment and eventually died in detention in 1987. Julius Streicher was convicted of crimes against humanity and acquitted of crimes against peace. He was sentenced to death and was executed within weeks of the final judgment. In other words, when the judges came to impose the "supreme penalty", aggressive war no longer figured as the "supreme crime".

The debate that went on during 1944 and early 1945 about the criminalization of aggressive war appears to have been influenced by concern that the highest leaders of the Nazi regime might go unpunished. Focusing on war crimes as they had been defined traditionally ran the risk that soldiers at the lowest level and their immediate commanders would become the targets of prosecution, but that it would be difficult to follow the chain up to the higher levels. The defendants at the Leipzig trials were commanders of U-boats and prisoner-of-war camps, not admirals and generals. Contemporary international criminal law has developed techniques to facilitate the conviction of those in the upper level of the hierarchy of evil, such as the concept of command or superior responsibility[52] and that of "joint criminal enterprise" complicity.[53] Although the origins of the two techniques can be traced to the post-Second World War jurisprudence, little or no thought had been given to them by the experts assembled in London in 1944 and 1945. The prospect of tracing a chain of criminal liability for war crimes up through the ranks from an SS commander in Normandy to the high command in Berlin must have seemed

---

[50] See, for example: *International Covenant on Civil and Political Rights*, (1976) 999 UNTS 171, art. 4(2).
[51] On this point, see Röling's observations, *supra* note 49, at pp. 67, 99.
[52] For example, *Rome Statute of the International Criminal Court*, *supra* note 2, art. 28.
[53] *Prosecutor* v. *Tadic* (Case No. IT-94-1-A), Judgment, 15 July 1999, para. 677.

daunting indeed, although in the end it did not prove to be too great a problem for prosecutors.

Aggressive war was a kind of prosecutorial magic bullet capable of ensuring the conviction of those at the very top. Even today, we remain perplexed by the due process issues involved in concluding that aggressive war has taken place because it appears to mean a more or less automatic finding of guilt for an entire stratum of senior officials. That the decision *Concl* may be taken by a political body (such as the Security Council) and not be reviewable in any genuine sense by a court of law is particularly disturbing. But in 1944 and 1945, plans for prosecution were an unembarrassed mixture of the political and the judicial. The goal of the United Nations War Crimes Commission and of the London Conference was to punish the Nazis, and criminalization of aggressive war seemed the most secure way for this to take place. The mood was very different from that of the Rome *Rome* Conference in 1998, which renounced any possibility of prosecuting past crimes,[54] and sought only to create a scheme that would govern conduct in the future, although it would be an overstatement to claim there were no political agendas at Rome.

The conclusion that the "supreme international crime" jargon of the judges at Nuremberg may have been a bit of judicial hyperbole is not in any way intended to trivialize the importance of punishment of aggression. But it is certainly striking to observe that the uncertainty about the role of aggression within the overall system of international criminal law is not only characteristic of the debate that immediately preceded Nuremberg, but it is also manifested in the approach to the issue in the decades that were to follow the landmark trial. The failure of the United Nations War Crimes Commission to even take a position on whether or not aggressive war should be a crime[55] seems remarkably like the hesitations at the Rome Conference, more than half a century later. After haunting the corridors of the FAO building for weeks, aggression was finally slipped in to the final package submitted by the Bureau to the Committee of the Whole of the Diplomatic Conference on 17 July 1998, but only barely. And there is still no guarantee that its presence in article 5(1) may only be pure symbolism.

[54] *Rome Statute of the International Criminal Court, supra* note 2, art. 11.
[55] Eventually, the United Nations War Crimes Commission did take a position on the subject, but only after the London Conference. A resolution adopted on 30 January 1946 declared that "crimes against peace and crimes against humanity, as referred to in the Four Power Agreement of August 8th, 1946 (i.e. the Nuremberg Charter), were war crimes within the jurisdiction of the Commission". See United Nations War Crimes Commission, *supra* note 11, p. 187.

There is perhaps one major difference between the 1944 debate and today's discussions. In 1944-1945 the experts were clear about whom they wanted to punish, but unsure whether this was consistent with principles of international law and the general maxim *nullum crimen sine lege*. At the dawn of the twenty-first century, there is less concern with the latter, and rather more with the potential targets of prosecutions for aggression. We live at a time when one superpower dominates international relations in both a political and a military sense. It possesses the most powerful armed force in history, one that dwarfs those of its nearest rivals and friends, and it is undaunted in its determination to use force or its threat in the pursuit of national policy. Such a context makes it difficult indeed to reach a consensus definition of the crime of aggression and on the conditions under which it may be prosecuted. During previous attempts at codification, in 1944-1945 as well as in 1919, context was of paramount significance. Perhaps the most useful historical lesson is that we should not lose sight of the fact that this is as true today as it was then.

3. Will Aggressors Ever be Tried Before the ICC?

MUHAMMAD AZIZ SHUKRI[*]

"Aggression" Between the Nuremberg Tribunal and the Rome Statute

Over fifty years ago, it was authoritatively held by the International Military Tribunal (IMT) at Nuremberg that initiating a war of aggression was the supreme international crime. According to Professor Benjamin B. Ferencz, at that time there was "no agreed definition of what was meant by aggression". Yet the validity of the IMT's conclusion has never been successfully challenged or refuted. The First General Assembly of the U.N unanimously affirmed both the Charter and Judgment condemning "Crimes against Peace". Hence, to use the words of Chief Justice of the U.S.A., Robert M. Jackson, armed aggression became an "international crime instead of a national right".

Let us recall that the Charter of the IMT to a certain extent, spelled out, the elements of the *crime against peace*, which was tantamount to aggression. The Tribunal considered the following acts as crime against peace, namely; "planning, preparation, initiation or waging of a war of aggression or a war in violation of international treaties, agreements or assurances or participation in a common plan or conspiracy for the accomplishment of any of the foregoing" (*U.N. Treaty Series 1951,* p. 288).

These guidelines have enlightened both the jurists and politicians who have, since the League of Nations been engaged in finding a generally agreed upon definition of *aggression*. In particular the Charter of the U.N. which is considered the constitution of international relations since the end of WWII although referring to aggressions, combating aggression and authorizing the Security Council under Chapter VII to determine the existence of "Act of Aggression", has nowhere stipulated what aggression

---

[*] Professor of International Law, University of Damascus.

actually meant. One has to reconcile himself with the fact that in Article 39 and Article 2, para. 4 any use of force or threat to the peace, let alone aggression were most emphatically denounced. In fact, the Charter, it could be conveniently argued, allowed the use of force in two *exclusive cases*, self-defense under Article 51, and the use of force under the banner of the U.N. according to the theory of *collective security* (i.e. Chapter VII). In fact self-defense in its restrictive way (*stricto sensu*) specified in Article 51 or in its *lato sensu*, i.e. anticipatory self-defense, have become well established by the practice of the overwhelming majority of States. An ultra liberal interpretation of so called self defense has been manifested in certain military actions taken illegally against some States on the ground that an attack on a citizen or an interest of a State regardless of the place of the attack had been considered aggression (e.g. the attack on Libya as a revenge for the alleged Libyan involvement of the disco incident in Berlin), and most recently the missile attack on the Sudanese pharmaceutical factory in revenge for the attack on the American embassies in Dar Es Salaam and Nairobi and the wanton attack on Afghanistan in an attempt to get the famous or infamous Osama Bin Laden). I cannot accept this view or these acts of aggressions both in morality and in law. To me, these are typical examples of cases of aggression disguised under a variety of headings, such as, self help, retaliation or combating so-called terrorism (terrorism has never found an appropriate definition since the *terror mania* began in September 1972 up till now).

Any other use of force in my mind is outlawed in the Charter, particularly what is known, in our days, as intervention for *humanitarian reasons*. Such interventions can be justified only if allowed or at least unequivocally blessed by the Security Council. This is how I read Resolution 2625 (XXXV) of the General Assembly. This Resolution, in a crystal clear manner, provides, *inter alia*, that:

> Every state has the duty to refrain in its international relations from the threat or use of force against the territorial integrity or political independence of any state or any other manner inconsistent with the purposes of the U.N. Such a threat or use of force constitutes a violation of international law and the Charter of the United Nations and shall never be employed as a means of settling international issues.
>
> A war of aggression constitutes a crime against the peace for which there is responsibility under international law.
>
> Nothing in the foregoing paragraphs shall be construed as enlarging or diminishing in any way the scope of the provisions of the Charter concerning cases in which the use of force is lawful.

Most importantly, at this juncture, the resolution goes on to stipulate that:

> No State or groups of States has the right to intervene directly or indirectly, *for any reason whatever*, in the internal or external affairs of any other State. Consequently, *armed intervention* and *all other forms of interference* or attempted threats against the personality of the State or against its political, economic and cultural elements *are in violation of international law.*

Fortunately, on December 14, 1974, the General Assembly of the United Nations, after over twenty years of hard work, approved by consensus, Resolution No. 3314 (XXIX) which contained a definition of aggression. This definition has been acknowledged both by jurisprudence and doctrine, i.e. the most highly qualified publicists in all four corners of the world.

On the other hand, the International Court of Justice considered that that definition reflected customary international law. Justice Stephen Schwebel, the President of the ICJ who at a time was the U.S. Representative to the Special Committee on the question of defining aggression asserted that Resolution 3314 is rather "an interpretation by the General Assembly of the meaning of the provisions of the U.N. Charter governing the use of armed force … in contravention of the Charter…as such of itself it is significant". I could hardly find a textbook on international law or on international criminal law, where Resolution 3314 is not fully quoted as the authoritative and generally agreed upon definition of aggression. True, technically speaking, said resolution was a *recommendation.* True, it had many political elements in it. But one may equally add that politics cannot be separated from international law. International law, I have always contended, is the by-product of politics. Further and above, can we not agree with Judge Rosalyn Higgins that the Resolutions of the General Assembly, at times, declare customary international law? One may quote many such resolutions such as 1415 of 1960 and 2625 of 1970, etc. as cases in point. In fact, the International Court of Justice in the case of *Nicaragua v. US* in 1986 stated that Resolution 3314 declared customary international law. Any attempt on the part of some publicists to divide Resolution 3314 into parts and pieces some with customary values and some without is an unacceptable intellectual exercise no more and no less. On the other hand, to argue that Resolution 3314 of 1974 determined the responsibility of States not the criminality of individuals is a good show of playing with words.

Aggression as a crime cannot be committed save by natural persons, even though such persons would be acting in their official capacity as politico-military leaders of a State or a group of States.

When the International Law Commission presented its Draft for the Statute of International Criminal Court, it included aggression among the crimes falling within the jurisdiction of the Court. It defined aggression as follows:

> Aggression means an act committed by an individual who as a leader or organizer is involved in the use of armed force by a state against the territorial integrity or political independence of another state, or in any other manner inconsistent with the Charter of the U.N.

Alternatively;

> The crime of aggression is committed by a person who is in a position of exercising control or capable of directing political/military actions in his State against another state in contravention to the Charter of the U.N. by resorting to armed force, to threaten or violate that State's sovereignty, territorial integrity or political independence.
>
> Acts constituting aggression include the following (the list indicated in para. 3 of Resolution 3314, 1974 [*The Statute of the International Criminal Court, A Documentary History*, compiled by M. Cherif Bassiouni, 1998; Transnational Publishers, Inc., Ardsley, N.Y. 1998 Pages 469-470].

Before the U.N. Diplomatic Conference of Plenipotentiaries on the Establishment of an International Criminal Court, the Preparatory Commission, while maintaining the crime of aggression as one of the crimes falling within the jurisdiction of the forthcoming court left three options for the member States to choose for the definition of aggression. It stated as an introductory note, the following: "This draft is without prejudice to the discussion of the issue of the relationship of the Security Council with the International Criminal Court with respect to aggression as dealt with in Article 10 (of the drafted Statute)." The first option followed a generic approach, i.e. a general definition of aggression as stated in Article 1 of Resolution 3314 while converting the text of said Resolution to fit the act of the individuals committing that crime. Option two, on the other hand, practically copied Resolution 3314 including the list included therein. The third option confined aggression to the use of force *amounting to the establishment of a military occupation of or annexing the territory of another state or part thereof by the armed forces of the attacking state.*

The three options were heatedly debated in Rome but without reaching any decisive conclusion. And the crime of aggression, as a result, was practically dropped from the Draft Statute two days before the conclusion of the Conference. Thanks to the strong intervention by the non-aligned movement backed by some other European States, aggression was re-installed in the Statute a few hours before the conclusion of the Conference by including the crime in Article 5 as one of those crimes falling within the jurisdiction of the court together with the crime of genocide, crimes against humanity and war crimes. There was, however, a considerable distinction between the crime of aggression and other crimes. For all the other crimes, the jurisdiction of the court shall commence upon the entry of the Statute into force. Whereas, according to para. 2 of Article 5: "The Court shall exercise jurisdiction over the crime of aggression once a provision is adopted in accordance with Articles 121 and 123 defining the crime and setting out the conditions under which the Court shall exercise jurisdiction with respect to this crime. Such a provision shall be consistent with the relevant provisions of the Charter of the U.N."

'Aggression' in the First Seven Sessions of the Preparatory Commission for Establishing the International Criminal Court

When the Preparatory Commission established by the final act of the Rome Conference held its first session (16-26 February 1999) in New York it was supposed to be fully engaged with two major issues, the Elements of Crime and the Rules of Procedure and Evidence. The Arab group supported by a few other States, particularly those from the Non-Aligned Movement raised the issue of aggression, but their cry was not readily heeded on the ground that the Mandate of the Commission, priority wise, was to focus on the above-mentioned two issues. However, Syria joined by Bahrain, Iraq, Lebanon, Libya, Oman, Sudan and Yemen on the very last day of that Session tabled Document PCNICC/1999/DP.11 in which they re-instated their understanding of the definition of aggression. It is noteworthy that this Document reflected to a great extent, Resolution 3314 of 1974 amended to include the attack on the right of people to self-determination as an act of aggression. The purpose of that move was merely to keep the subject of aggression on the agenda of the Preparatory Commission for its next Sessions. By the next Sessions and upon an increasing demand by NAM States, a Compilation of Proposals on the crime of aggression was submitted and old proposals which were submitted in Rome were revived again. The President of the Preparatory Commission, Ambassador Philippe Kirsch was persuaded by the Arab Ambassadors during the July-August 1999 Session, to give more attention to aggression. As a result, he appointed Mr. Tuvaku Manongi of Tanzania as a coordinator for the group on aggression and promised to devote every Monday throughout the coming sessions to debate aggression and its relation to the authority of the Security Council with regards to the jurisdiction of the International Criminal Court concerning this particular crime. He also encouraged both the coordinator and States concerned to engage in as many informal discussions as possible on the question.

During the July-August 1999 Session, the coordinator exerted little effort in his task. This was partly due to the reluctance of some delegates who were against having a solution to the two pending problems relating to the activation of the Court in adjudicating the perpetrators of aggression. On 2 August 1999, upon the insistence of the NAM Movement the Coordinator tabled a compilation of proposals on the crime of aggression. It included proposals submitted to the PrepCom on the Establishment of the International Criminal Court 1996–1998 before Rome, at the United Nations Diplomatic Conference of Plenipotentiaries on the Establishment of an International Criminal Court 1998, in Rome, and at the Preparatory Commission for the International Criminal Court since its first session in 1999 (PCNICC/1999/INF/2). There appeared yet another new document PCNICC/1999/DP/12 which carried a proposal submitted by the Russian Federation. This proposal is rather unique. It reads as follows:

> For the purposes of the present Statute and subject to a prior determination by the U.N. Security Council of an act of aggression by the State concerned, the crime of aggression means any of the following acts: planning, preparing, initiating, carrying out a war of aggression.

In Document PCNICC/1999/DP/13 of 30 July 1999, Germany re-introduced an old definition previously presented in Document A/AC.249/1998/DP12 of 1 April 1998. The German old/new definition concentrates on the element of the occupation of part or all of the territory of the aggressed State. Thus, it excluded, or may be interpreted to exclude, other forms of aggression listed in Resolution 3314. This was not acceptable to an increasing number of States. It should be added, however, that the components of Resolution 3314 were not and still are not fully accepted by a number of States on various grounds.

During the next Session, November–December 1999, on December 9, the coordinator presented a Discussion Paper containing a preliminary attempt to coordinate the proposals thus far submitted for:

-   The Definition of the Crime of Aggression;

-   The Conditions under which the Court shall exercise Jurisdiction and the role of the U.N. Security Council at this juncture.

It is noteworthy that with regard to the first problem, i.e. the definition, the coordinator presented several options which virtually reflected the three approaches thus far surfacing before, during and after the Rome Conference, I mean a generic definition, a list definition based on Resolution 3314 and a restrictive definition confining aggression to the case of the occupation, partly or fully of the territory of the victim state. Under one of the options, he merely repeated the Russian proposal. This all indicates, to my mind, that *the real problem here, as always, is not the definition of aggression however important this may be.* It is rather the problem of the relations between the ICC and the Security Council if the ICC ever wants to exercise its function regarding the crime of aggression. That difficulty was underlined by the coordinator's second report of 29 March 2000, PCNICC/2000/WGCA/ART1 in which he rightly stated the following, *inter alia*:

I. Possible issues relating to the Rome Statute

Definition

Whether the definition should be more general in nature referring to what may be the essential characteristics of the crime of aggression. (Possible instruments of reference: Charter of the United Nations; Nuremburg Charter; Draft Code of Crimes against the Peace and Security of Mankind; case law and other documents)

Whether the definition should include a more specific list of acts that could constitute the crime of aggression. (Possible instrument of reference: General Assembly resolution 3314 (XXIX))

Whether it would be possible to identify some acts listed in resolution 3314 (XXIX) and add them to the general definition of the crime of aggression.

Conditions under which the Court shall exercise jurisdiction

The report of the coordinator stated the following:

> What role should be played by the Security Council in relation to the jurisdiction of the Court over the crime of aggression?
>
> What action, if any, could be taken in the event that the Security Council fails or otherwise declines to determine that an act of aggression has occurred?
>
> What are the legal effects on the functions of the Court arising from a determination by the Council that an act of aggression was committed by a State?

The coordinator goes on to list many other issues which, to the minds of many delegates, including myself are not relevant for this debate, such as the general principle of criminal law or the possible issues relating to the elements of the crime of aggression or the possible issues relating to the rules of procedure and evidence. In my opinion, the only issues of immediate concern are: 1. definition, 2. conditions under which the Court shall exercise jurisdiction.

Similar feelings were expressed in a very intriguing paper presented on 24 March by Professor Mauro Politi of Italy (PCNICC/2000/WGCA/DP3). This paper attempted, in a very methodological way, to set the ground for a fruitful negotiation on the pending problems. I do hope it will receive our best attention at this end and at other meetings focusing on aggression.

At this point, one cannot but admire such newly tabled proposals such as those presented by Colombia, PCNICC/2000/1GCA/DP1/AD1 of 17 March 2000 and the very elegant ideas contained in the paper from Greece and Portugal PCNICC/1999/WGCA/DP1 of 7 December 1999. These two proposals together with an earlier proposal by Cameroon A/CONF183/C.1/L39 dealt with the two problems together, as the case should be. During the seven sessions of the PrepCom another new proposal on aggression was tabled on 23 February 2001 by Bosnia and Herzegovina, New Zealand and Romania (PCNICC/2001/WGCA/DP.1). All the previous proposals, particularly the Greek–Portuguese, the Bosnia and Herzegovina and others attempted, each in its own way, to get around the problem of the Security Council refusing or failing to characterize the situation before it as aggression. To me, the Greek-Portuguese proposal, thus far, looks the closest to my personal approach and to the view of the Arab States on behalf of which I have been speaking during the last seven PrepCom Sessions if not to the NAM Group, assuming the latter can be said to have one unified stand on the Rome Statute altogether.

We also now have a new coordinator, Ms. Silvia Fernandez de Gurmendi from Argentina. I am hopeful that she will receive more help from the parties concerned than her predecessor. I am also sure that she would realize the significance of making a breakthrough on this sensitive crime before the Prep Com concludes its sessions. Frankly speaking, a number of States will base their attitude toward ratifying the Rome Statute on this very question!

In conclusion, with regard to the definition, I would repeat what I stated on 6 December 1999, that the perpetrator of aggression is the leader or leaders or high ranking officers of a State or States who are in a position to exercise control or capable of directing political or military actions in his or their States against another State or States in contravention of the rules of international law, particularly those stated in the Charter of the U.N. Such aggression includes initiation, planning, preparing, ordering, carrying out or conspiring to commit such a heinous offence. Any definition which meets these elements, is acceptable to me as a scholar of international criminal law. As blunt as I am known to be, let us not here confuse the issues by giving illusive cases such as skirmishes on the border or simple exchange of fire as one form of aggression or another. They are not. Aggression is known to almost any scholar of law, let alone the judges sitting on the bench of ICC who according to the Rome Statute will hopefully be of the highest caliber in both international and criminal law from all major legal systems of the world. It might be useful to remember that Adolph Hess was justly indicted and sentenced to life imprisonment and died in disgrace for committing only the crime of aggression. Mind you, aggression was not then defined meticulously the way we are seeking to do now.

With regard to the inter-relationship between the Security Council and the Court, there has never been a denial on the part of any delegation in Rome or in the Preparatory Commission meetings that the Security Council, by the Charter of the United Nations is the primary organ in determining the existence of a state of aggression. How can we dispute a prerogative given by the Constitution of International Relations to this principal *executive organ* of the U.N., i.e. the Security Council. We have always questioned what the case would be if we found a utopian definition of aggression, but the Council, due to a veto by one of its five permanent members, failed to act either because the aggressor was one of the big five or an ally or a friend of the same! My early proposal to implement the Uniting for Peace Resolution was readily refused by the very States which passed it in 1950 and defended it so strongly for decades! It further invoked that famous Resolution on more than one occasion. Yet, that same Resolution is now invalid, impractical and to some even illegal. Is this not a mockery?

Shall we therefore give up and let the act of aggression be committed without the perpetrator being brought to justice? Or shall we have a kind of fall back to deal with such situations? Many proposals have been tabled to answer my questions, and I don't think I will improve the situation by adding another. Nevertheless, I may say, that the insistence shown by more than one of the big five to assiduously and stubbornly preserve the role of the Security Council as the *only* trigger to activate the Court with regard to the crime of aggression remains the real formidable problem, which should be addressed rationally, objectively and pragmatically. I dare say that many of the constructive ideas aired at this juncture are worth serious consideration.

Last but not least, it is a real pity to keep ourselves busy trying small and medium-size fishes while ignoring the big sharks that are the real threat to the human race simply because of pure political considerations. Should this be allowed to happen, the International Criminal Court will not, I am afraid, be the great achievement we thought we had made on 17 July 1998, and International Humanitarian Law will still be far from achieving its ambition because aggressors will not be easily brought before this august judicial body. Is that what we all aspire to cultivate? I surely hope not.

4. The Debate within the Preparatory Commission for the International Criminal Court

MAURO POLITI[*]

1.

The purpose of this meeting is to stimulate a frank and informal debate on the question of the crime of aggression, which remains a formidable challenge. Many of the participants in the meeting are veterans of the negotiations that took place before and during the Rome Conference, and at the Preparatory Commission. They have experienced the difficulties in advancing a process that is not only intricate from a legal standpoint, but also strongly influenced by political factors and concerns. From the beginning, this combination has resulted in some of the most heated arguments heard during the ICC process. What we in Trento intended to do is to provide a different and more relaxed forum for exchanging views and confronting ideas between academics and negotiators, and among negotiators. We thought that giving this opportunity to experts could help both reflecting on problems and facilitating the dialogue. We do not have other ambitions. The magic formulas and compromises that would hopefully allow the question of aggression to be resolved will be found elsewhere, within the competent bodies. But even if we only manage to achieve a better understanding of the legal and also the political framework relating to the crime of aggression, our meeting could be considered successful.

---

[*] Professor of International Law, University of Trento.

2.

My task is to speak about aggression and the works of the Preparatory Commission. In other words, to complete the picture of where we stand on the questions left unresolved by Article 5 of the Rome Statute. What I am expected to do is to summarize the proposals made both on the definition of the crime of aggression and on the conditions for the Court's intervention; to outline the main trends and developments in the discussion; to assess the prospects for progress of the exercise. Due to a number of reasons, however, the assignment is perhaps not as simple as it may appear. The dynamics of the negotiations within the PrepCom have been rather complex, with a frequent alternance of discussions of substance and sessions devoted to procedure, namely the best way to channel and structure the debate. Signs of encouraging progress have often been followed by moments of total stalemate and vice versa. The active participation of delegates to the meetings on aggression has been varied and only recently can one say that a sufficiently broad range of views and positions have been expressed. All these factors concur in somehow complicating the effort to distill the sense of what has happened so far.

3.

With this warning, and trying to be concise, I think that the debate within the Preparatory Commission went through three phases: the first one, characterized by a prevalence of procedural arguments and manoeuvers; the second, where the focus was mainly on rationalizing the debate and putting together the text of existing options and proposals; and a third phase in which the interest turned to discussing the merit of some specific suggestions.

The first phase went from the beginning of the work of the PrepCom in February 1999 until the end of the second session in August 1999. The priority, at that time, was to complete the rules of procedure and the elements of crimes. Also, the Rome Conference had not set a final term for the Commission to complement the provisions of the Statute on aggression. The debate suffered then from lack of sufficient time available and often resulted in a repetition of well-known positions of principle. One of the most controversial issue was whether to establish a special Working Group devoted to this crime. Some long procedural discussions took place on this point, which were again evidence of the fierce contrasts that remained after Rome on fundamental questions.

On the one hand, the main concern of the "great powers" (and permanent members of the Security Council) was that the Court could be used as a "resonance box" of propaganda – attacks against the use of force even when such use was fully consistent with the Charter of the U.N. For these countries, there was no special urgency in addressing the crime of aggression; in any case, the crime should have been defined in a restrictive manner, in line with existing customary law. It was also essential that the Court's jurisdiction to assess individual criminal responsibility was made dependent upon a decision of the Security Council on the existence of an aggression by a State. On the contrary, other countries (especially from the developing world) insisted on defining as soon and as widely as possible the notion of a crime of which they felt they were often the victims; and feared that failing to provide a specific forum (like a WG) would make the question fall into oblivion. Moreover, they wanted to avoid any undue interference of the Security Council in the future activity of the Court in this area. The WG on aggression was eventually established, still with limited time allocated to it. But, if we look at substance, no significant progress was made, aside from agreeing on producing a compilation of all the various proposals related to aggression.

The second phase covers the three sessions of the PrepCom from December 1999 until 30 June 2000, when both the rules of procedure and the elements of crimes were finalized. The trend became more encouraging, although in a context where ideological positions remained predominant and participation to the debates was still limited to a sort of club of "aficionados". In particular, there were some serious attempts to rationalize the debate. A consolidated text of the various options, both on definition and on the relationships with the Security Council, was produced by the WG. A few crucial questions were also identified with the idea of addressing them in a given order (this was described as the "thematic approach" to the issue of aggression). A list of questions was proposed by the coordinator as a guideline for future work. One must admit that the thematic approach was not always coherently followed by delegates. But these decisions on methods of work had somehow a positive impact on the discussions on substance, which became more focused and concrete, also thanks to new proposals that showed the efforts to seek ways to bridge gaps in a pragmatic manner.

After June 2000 we had two more sessions of the PrepCom, the last one held in February-March 2001. With regard to aggression, this third phase took advantage of various factors. First, the conclusion of the work on the rules of procedure and on the elements allowed the Bureau to allocate more time to the special Working Group. Second, and due again to the fact that other important documents had been finalized, the interest of a greater number of delegations turned to the question of aggression, and participation in the debate increased considerably. Third, the coordinators of the WG (Tuvaku Manongi and then Silvia Fernandez de Gurmendi) managed to concentrate the discussion on specific texts, in particular a Greek-Portuguese proposal on both definition and conditions and a proposal from Bosnia and Herzegovina, New Zealand and Romania on the relationships with the Security Council.[1] As I will try to explain in a moment, we are still far from seeing the light at the end of the tunnel, and fundamental differences remain; but, in my view at least, these developments authorize a cautious optimism on the positive outcome of the work on aggression.

4.

Turning to substance, my remarks will be limited to a few essential points, to be used as a background for our discussion, especially to the benefit of those who did not participate in the work of the PrepCom. Other colleagues, I am sure, will go much deeper into the various issues.

Under Article 5 of the Statute, and the Final Act of the Rome Conference, the task of the PrepCom is twofold: to define the crime of aggression and to set out the conditions under which the Court shall exercise jurisdiction with respect to this crime. When we speak about conditions, we intend to refer essentially to the relationships between the Court and the Security Council: namely to the issue of if, and to what extent, the functions of the Court with regard to the crime of aggression will depend upon the determination by the Security Council, under article 39 of the U.N. Charter, that a State has committed aggression. On both aspects, there are numerous options still open.

Let me start from definition. There is one element on which everybody seems to agree: that the crime of aggression is a leadership crime. In other words, it is a crime to be restricted to acts committed by state officials, particularly by those individuals in a position of political or military leadership or who are otherwise the organizers or planners of acts constituting aggression. Thus, aggression is a crime perpetrated by those who have decision–making power on behalf of a State. It is not a crime that

---

[1]   The texts of both proposals can be read in the U.N. website regarding the ICC (see the Editors' Preface, above).

can be committed by people acting in a private capacity, or by low-level political or military officials of a State. This is a point of convergence among the various proposals, which is duly reflected in the consolidated text.

But the main issue remains unresolved: how should we define the crime of aggression for the purposes of the ICC Statute? One suggestion is based on the opinion that the prohibition in existing customary law relates only to the planning, preparation, initiation or waging of a "war of aggression", as provided in the Nuremberg Charter (proposals originally made by France and the Russian Federation in 1996). A second option is to provide a general definition of the crime of aggression, centered on the concept of the use of armed force against the sovereignty, territorial integrity or political independence of a State in violation of the U.N. Charter (proposals by Denmark, Greece and Finland of 1996, by Cameroon of 1998, by Greece and Portugal of 1999 and 2000, by Colombia of 2000). Under a third option, the general definition should be accompanied by a non exhaustive list of acts constituting aggression, taken from G.A. resolution 3314 of 1974, to be regarded as an authoritative source of existing law also for the purposes of the ICC Statute (proposal by Egypt and Italy of 1997, proposal by a group of Arab countries of 1998, which also adds to the general definition the concept of use of force aimed at depriving other people of their rights of self-determination). Finally, the consolidated text includes a German proposal, reiterated in 1999, whose main thrust was to link the commission of the crime of aggression to the circumstance that the armed attack by a State had the object or the effect of a military occupation or of an annexation of the territory of another State. The intent was to cover the most obvious cases of aggression, while avoiding entering the debate on the other types of acts listed in resolution 3314. A further German paper of November 2000 reaffirmed, in this respect, that the essence of the crime of aggression presupposes a large-scale, aggressive armed attack on the territorial integrity of another State, clearly without justification under international law.

It would be impossible to give here an account of all the arguments brought in favor of the different options. But most of these arguments revolve around one fundamental question: what is today the content of customary international law relating to the crime of aggression? Is it still the one reflected in the Nuremberg Charter, which refers to a full-scale war of aggression, or has it developed up to the point of also including other acts of aggression? What is the value, in this regard (and thus for purposes of individual criminal responsibility), of precedents such as resolution

3314, but also the 1986 ICJ judgment on the *Nicaragua* case which recognized the customary nature of at least one of the provisions of such resolution? What is the relevance of the 1996 ILC Draft Code of Crimes against the Peace and Security of Mankind, which contains a general definition of aggression? Other points were repeatedly made: for example, that agreeing on a general definition could prove to be easier giving the sensitive political nature of the issues involved. Moreover, it was said that such definition would give the Court the necessary flexibility in assessing whether an act would present the characteristics and the gravity to be regarded as a crime of aggression. On the other hand, the sponsors of the definition based on resolution 3314 underlined the need for respecting the principle of legality, as it was done with regard to the other crimes covered by the Statute. Now, I think we should ask ourselves: would a greater discretion in this area really give the Court a better chance to prosecute and punish the crime of aggression? Or would it increase the risks of politically motivated complaints and of incoherence in the Court's jurisprudence? And vice versa, can we say that the principle of legality is respected in international criminal law only when the constituent elements of the crime involved are set out in detail by the relevant legislation? Together with the one on the content of customary law, these are the main questions waiting for answers in the process of defining the crime of aggression.

I am confident about our chances of reaching an agreement on definition at the PrepCom. From what I have seen, positions are distant, but not too distant. There is now a greater margin of flexibility in the position of the champions of opposite views, and many of them have indicated that they are ready to consider different solutions than the one that they advocate. In other words, definition is probably not the most troubling obstacle to completing the work on aggression.

5.

The main problem is instead the relationships with the Security Council. The reason is evident. This is indeed a problem that touches upon the institutional balance between the judiciary functions of the Court and the political prerogatives of the Council under the U.N. Charter. Accordingly, it involves issues of interpretation of fundamental provisions of the Charter and of the Rome Statute. It affects considerably the character and the degree of independence of the Court.

The consolidated text of 1999 reflects these difficulties, and shows in particular a sharp division between extreme positions: namely, on the one side, the position that the Court should be able to proceed regardless of any determination by the Council on the existence of a State aggression, and the position that such a determination is always a prerequisite for the Court to consider the commission of this crime. Luckily things have evolved since 1999. There seems to be an agreement today at least on the point that there cannot be individual responsibility for the crime of aggression unless the State concerned has international responsibility for aggression. Now, to determine that a State has committed an act of aggression remains within the prerogatives of the Security Council, under article 39 of the U.N. Charter. And this leads to the conclusion, which I repeat appears to be widely accepted, that in principle the Court may come into play only once the Council has decided that the State concerned has committed aggression.

The real difficulties arise when we consider two other aspects. First, what should be the legal effects of the Council's determination on the functions of the Court? Secondly, what happens in the event that the Council fails or otherwise declines to determine that an aggression by a State has occurred? On these key issues, opinions are divided and there is still plenty of work to do for the PrepCom.

On the effects of the Council's determination (naturally when this determination is actually made), we are facing a clear alternative. In other words, should the Council's decision be construed as a procedural condition, or should it be considered also binding on the Court as regards the commission of aggression by a State? It seems clear that the first option (procedural condition) would be more respectful of the judicial independence of the Court. The Court would be free to establish in each case all aspects of individual criminal responsibility, namely whether an act of aggression took place and whether the accused was in this respect a leader, planner or organizer. The importance of having a definition (and possibly a detailed definition) of the crime of aggression would become paramount. In fact, the Court could determine for instance that an act of aggression took place on different grounds than the ones considered by the Council, and it could also deny, for purposes of individual criminal responsibility, the existence of an act of aggression.

Vice versa, to make the Council's decision binding on the Court would certainly help avoid inconsistency between the determinations of the two organs, but then the Court would be left to decide only upon the degree of participation of the accused in the activity of the State. And somebody has also pointed out that, in this case, we do not even need a definition of the crime of aggression, since aggression would simply be what the

Security Council has determined as such. These points have been discussed here and there within the PrepCom, but I think are very relevant points in need of being further debated and clarified.

Finally, how should we deal with the situation in which the Security Council fails to determine that a State aggression has occurred? We know that this situation could be very frequent. History shows that the Council is very reluctant to say that an aggression took place. The use or threat of veto by the permanent members increases the likelihood of no decision being made by the Council.

Now, the Preparatory Commission has given considerable attention to this issue, especially during the last sessions. There is an obvious resistance from the P/5 to accept any solution that would allow the Court to proceed without a previous decision by the Council. The "primary" responsibility for the maintenance of international peace and security given to the Council by Article 24 of the U.N. Charter is interpreted as an "exclusive" responsibility. Instead, a number of proposals go in a different direction, in an effort to find ways to balance the prerogatives of the Council with the effectiveness of the Court. I refer, in particular, to the Greek-Portuguese text and to the proposal submitted by Bosnia and Herzegovina, New Zealand and Romania.

The Greek-Portuguese text is quite simple and straightforward. It provides that, in the presence of a complaint related to the crime of aggression, the Court will first inquire whether the Council has made any determination relating to the alleged aggression by a State. If this is not the case, the Court will ask the Council to make a determination, but then it may nonetheless proceed once a period of 12 months has expired without a Council's decision or a Council's request to defer the investigation. In other words, the principle of the need for a previous determination by the Council is reaffirmed, but there would be an important exception to this principle. In fact, failure from the Council to act triggers the possibility for the Court to proceed. The independence and effectiveness of the Court is fully safeguarded, but one can also understand why so far this proposal has been strongly opposed by the permanent members of the Security Council.

On the other hand, the text submitted by Bosnia and Herzegovina, New Zealand and Romania is more complex. It involves in the process also the U.N. General Assembly and the International Court of Justice. Its main thrust, I believe, is to envisage a political and legal process that would guarantee a fair assessment of the occurrence of a State aggression in case of failure by the Council to make a determination. In essence, the text provides that, after 12 months from a notification by the Court without a Council's determination, the ICC may invite the General Assembly to request the ICJ to give an advisory opinion on the existence of an act of aggression by a State. And the Prosecutor may then proceed if the opinion of the ICJ is that there has been a case of aggression and the General Assembly recommends to go ahead. A complex and articulated procedure, I said, which raised a lot of interest among delegations, together with questions such as its consistency with Article 96 of the U.N. Charter, the amount of time required before the Court may act, the same legitimacy of having a role for the ICJ in the process. In any event, together with the Greek-Portuguese suggestion, this proposal is evidence of the fact that there are in place various imaginative attempts to resolve what is probably the most intricate and delicate issue at stake.

6.

I have some difficulties in drawing conclusions from this succinct outline of the work of the PrepCom on the crime of aggression. My intent is only to stimulate the debate on the points that I have briefly indicated. But let me say that, despite all the odds, there is now a widespread conviction among delegates of the need to find a way out that would allow the Court to repress one of the most serious crimes of concern to the international community. Perhaps the mission is not so impossible as it appeared two years ago. Also, everybody realizes that reaching agreement on the crime of aggression will be extremely important for the entire ICC process. Many countries are looking carefully at the developments concerning aggression, and a successful outcome in this area could be greatly beneficial to achieving the universality of the Court. Now the Commission has time and opportunity to tackle the question of aggression with the necessary intensity. And the dialogue is indeed open, thanks especially to the contribution of those delegates who are present here today. I hope that this gathering in Trento will result in another small step towards mutual understanding and progress in making the Court operational also with regard to the crime of aggression.

THE INTERNATIONAL CRIMINAL COURT AND THE CRIME OF AGGRESSION: QUESTIONS OF DEFINITION AND JURISDICTION

5. The Definition of the Crime of Aggression and the ICC Jurisdiction over that Crime

MOHAMMED M. GOMAA[*]

One hundred and sixty States participated in the United Nations Diplomatic Conference of Plenipotentiaries on the Establishment of an International Criminal Court held in Rome from 15 June to 17 July 1998[1] to draft the Statute of the International Criminal Court (ICC),[2] the establishment of which had been a challenge for the United Nations for more than 50 years. Those States made a last minute decision to confer upon the Court the "jurisdiction over the crime of aggression once a provision is adopted in accordance with Articles 121 and 123 defining the crime and setting out the conditions under which the Court shall exercise jurisdiction with respect to this crime".[3] They agreed to that compromise in order to secure the conclusion of the Statute after they had reached a deadlock over the crime "aggression".[4] The compromise led to the inclusion of aggression as one of

---

[*] B.A. and LL.B. (University of Cairo), *D.E.S.* and Ph.D. (University of Geneva). Legal Advisor to the Egyptian Delegation to the United Nations and member of the Egyptian Delegation in the Preparatory Commission for the Establishment of an International Criminal Court. The views expressed here are personal and do not necessarily reflect those of the Government of Egypt.

[1] 17 intergovernmental organizations, 14 specialized agencies and funds of the United Nations, as well as 124 non-governmental organizations also attended the Conference.

[2] Rome Statute, A/CONF, 183/9, 17 July 1998. The Statute was adopted by a non-recorded vote (requested by the United States) of 120 against 7 and 21 abstentions.

[3] Article 5 on "Crimes within the jurisdiction of the Court".

[4] By the last days of the Conference the picture was very somber. A comment by its bureau on the issue of aggression stated that if generally accepted provisions on its inclusion in the Statute were not developed by interested delegations by the close of 13 July 2001, it will propose that the interest in addressing these crimes be reflected in some other manner, for example, by a protocol or review conference. Press Release, L/ROM/16, 13 July 1998. Several delegations, particularly the representative of the European Union, supported the bureau's proposal. *Loc. cit.* However, other delegations, including Croatia, Egypt, Ghana, Iran and Syria considered unacceptable the non-inclusion of that crime, which was part of a decision by the Non-Aligned Movement in its recent ministerial meeting in Colombia.

the four crimes within the jurisdiction of the Court.[5] That was not without a price; it resulted in a main defect in the Statute. The Statute does not contain a readily applicable provision on aggression which, according to the whole international community, represented by the General Assembly, is "the gravest of all crimes against peace and security throughout the world",[6] without the punishment of which the ICC would not really become the ultimate long awaited international criminal jurisdiction.

Of course, the definition of aggression has always been an extremely difficult issue to settle. The history of the search for such a definition tells us that it is not a purely technical operation. Rather, it is overshadowed by political *bras de fer*. It has challenged the professionalism and patience of international negotiators for more than a century.[7] But, the negotiations over the ICC caused them to continue their plight in reaching a definition of aggression. According to Resolution "F" of the Diplomatic Conference[8] and in line with Article 5 of the Statute of the ICC, the Preparatory Commission for the International Criminal Court,

---

[5]   The other three are genocide, crimes against humanity and war crimes.

[6]   General Assembly Res. 380 (V) of 17 November, 1950. This is another paraphrasing of what the International Military Tribunal (IMT) at Nuremberg had coined as "the supreme international crime". I *Trial of the Major War Criminals before the International Military Tribunal*, Nuremberg, 1947, p. 186.

[7]   This is elaborated further below.

[8]   Resolution "F" stipulates that:

"*The United Nations Conference of Plenipotentiaries on the Establishment of an International Criminal Court,*

Having adopted the Statute of the International Criminal Court,

...

Decides as follows:

1. There is hereby established the Preparatory Commission for the International Criminal Court. ...

5. The Commission shall prepare proposals for practical arrangements for the establishment and coming into operation of the Court, including the draft texts of:

...

(b) Elements of Crimes;

...

7. The Commission shall prepare proposals for a provision on aggression, including the definition and Elements of Crimes of aggression and the conditions under which the International Criminal Court shall exercise its jurisdiction with regard to this crime. The Commission shall submit such proposals to the Assembly of States Parties at a Review Conference, with a view to arriving at an acceptable provision on the crime of aggression for inclusion in this Statute. The provisions relating to the crime of aggression shall enter into force for the States Parties in accordance with the relevant provisions of this Statute; ..."

established by that resolution, shall "prepare proposals for a provision on aggression, including the definition and Elements of Crimes of aggression and the conditions under which the International Criminal Court shall exercise its jurisdiction with regard to this crime. The Commission shall submit such proposals to the Assembly of States Parties at a Review Conference, with a view to arriving at an acceptable provision on the crime of aggression for inclusion in this Statute. The provisions relating to the crime of aggression shall enter into force for the States Parties in accordance with the relevant provisions of this Statute." Accordingly, the definition could only be considered for adoption at an amendment conference that cannot take place until more than seven years have elapsed after the Statute has gone into effect.[9]

This article seeks to determine whether the ICC needs to have a definition of aggression *of its own* or whether a definition under general international law is enough for the Court to undertake its tasks in connection with the crime of aggression. In so doing, it reconstructs the trail of the "definition of aggression" since its first and unsuccessful attempts until the adoption by the General Assembly of the only authoritative and agreed Definition of Aggression in 1974. It also analyzes the legal nature of the Definition of Aggression in order to prove its authority and adequacy.

The article further explores the question of the relationship between the International Criminal Court and the Security Council, with a view to clarifying the conditions for the exercise of the Court's jurisdiction over the crime of aggression.

Where to Start?

The preliminary question that we must ask ourselves at the outset is whether we are requested to – or whether we should – define aggression *de novo* for the purposes of the Statute of the ICC? or whether existing international law is adequate in this connection?

The Statute of the ICC is an international agreement consisting in objective law (prescribing rights and obligations). It is also a constitutional instrument (establishing the Court and defining its powers and procedures).

---

[9] Rome Statute, *supra* fn. 2, Articles 5, 121, 123 and 126. If the current pattern of ratification or accession continues, it would be expected that the Statute enter into force during 2002 upon its ratification by 60 States.

According to it, the jurisdiction of the Court *ratione personae* is confined to *individual criminal responsibility*. Thus, the Court cannot be seized with State responsibility as can, for example, the International Court of Justice.[10] As a corollary of this nature of the Statute a definition of aggression, for the purposes of the Court, should be one that has its *sedes materiae* not in the law of international responsibility (which applies to international persons not within the purview of the Court); rather it has to be found elsewhere: in criminal law (applied to the individual).

But the whole problem starts here. Aggression has particular features which distinguish it from the other crimes under the Statute. It is not a crime committed by individuals. It is an unlawful act which could only be committed by a collectivity. Therefore, aggression *per se* cannot be entertained directly by the ICC as it does not pertain *ratione personae* to individuals who come under its jurisdiction.

How then can we interpret Article 5 of the Statute on the definition of aggression? In fact, what contributes to the confusion caused by the drafting of that article is the phrase "a provision … defining the crime [of aggression]" in paragraph 2 of Article 5. It, therefore, needs to be determined what is exactly meant by it? Is it an invitation to define aggression for the purposes of the Statute of the ICC? More precisely, does it call for the provision of a *description* of what constitutes aggression? The analysis of the phrase, as well as literature and jurisprudence suggest negative answers to these questions.

The language of Article 5 is misleading. The literal meaning of "definition" is the description of a thing by its properties which helps in distinguishing it from others. So what we would be defining is "aggression" which is an unlawful act committed by a collectivity, which is not within the jurisdiction of the Court. Whence, by applying the rules of interpretation of treaties contained in Article 31 of the Vienna Convention on the Law of Treaties of 1969[11] the "ordinary" meaning of "definition" would lead to a legal absurdity since such a *definition* would not *in itself* enable the Court to undertake its judicial task. Therefore, a *definition stricto sensu* of aggression would not fulfill the legal requirements of Article 5 of the Statute.

---

[10]   Individual accountability, however, does not preclude international responsibility on the part of the international person as well, but that was a subject not dealt with in the Code of Offenses Against the Peace and Security of Mankind. *Cf.*, Article 4 and the commentary of Article 30 thereof, *YBILC*, II, Part Two, 1996, p. 23.

[11]   1155 *UNTS*, p. 331. Article 31 on the general rule on the interpretation of treaties stipulates that:

"1. A treaty shall be interpreted in good faith in accordance with the ordinary meaning to be given to the terms of the treaty in their context and in the light of its object and purpose."

Actually, the drafters of the Nuremberg and Tokyo Charters had confronted the same *problematique* more than 50 years ago. Before the Second World War, "aggression" could not be considered a crime under existing international law as it had not yet been defined.[12] As a consequence, individuals could not be held to account for it owing to the principle of legality expressed in the maxim *nullum crimen, nulla poena, sine previa lege poenali* (*nullum crimen sine lege*).[13] Therefore, the representatives of the four victors in the world war (the allied powers of USA – USSR – UK – France) embarked on a mission to define aggression for the purpose of individual criminal responsibility arising out of the events leading to the two landmark trials.[14] However, their initiative resulted in a different product as reflected in the original formula reached at London, which was far from a *definition* in the literal or legal sense, i.e., a description of what constitutes "aggression" or a "war of aggression" and what their elements were. Aggression was declared to be a "crime against peace"; but it was nowhere defined.

The London Formula

It was only after the Charter of the International Military Tribunal (IMT) at

---

[12] Crimes against peace and humanity, among which is aggression, have been criticized as *ex post facto* legislation on the part of the London Conference of 1945, in that these crimes did not exist in international law prior to that date. Judge Bert Roling of the International Military Tribunal for the Far East explained that aggressive war was not a crime under international law at the beginning of the war. It was an innovation of the Nuremberg and Tokyo trials. Cassese, Antonio, *The Tokyo Trial and Beyond: Reflections of a Peacemonger*, Cambridge, Polity Press, 993, p. 98.

[13] The prohibition of *ex post facto* law is rather new. It was introduced and generally accepted on the European continent through the French Revolution. "*Nullum crimen, nulla poena, sine previa lege poenali*" has nothing to do with Roman law. It was introduced relatively recently to further the principle of liberty and to protect citizens against the power of government. But even the Covenants of 1966, make a special exception for the cases in which the acts were criminal according to the "general principles of law recognized by the community of nations".

[14] The Nuremberg and Tokyo judgments contain an historical narrative of events upon which each of the two tribunals founded its conviction of the defendants of planning and engaging in aggressive war.

Nuremberg,[15] put together in London in 1945,[16] that aggression became an international crime and its perpetrators were prosecuted, tried and punished.[17] But what was the formula adopted in the Nuremberg Charter that led to the prosecution and punishment of the perpetrators? What was its legal significance? How did it function?

The representatives of the four Allied Powers convened in London from 26 June to 8 August 1945, at the International Conference on Military Trials[18] with a view to reaching a unified position on the law and procedure for what was to become the International Military Tribunal at Nuremberg. They were confronted with the most problematic and controversial issue of the *criminality* of aggressive war and the fact that aggression was a State-crime. Accordingly, they did not venture to introduce a crime of aggression committed by the individual *per se*. That led to their adoption of a formula that established the legal nexus between a "war of aggression" and the act of the individual implicated in it.

Article VI of the Charter of Nuremberg, which included aggression among the three categories of crimes that should come within the jurisdiction of the Nuremberg Tribunal, stipulated that:

---

[15] The Nuremberg Tribunal, which – like the Tokyo Tribunal – was set up by inter-Allied agreement at the end of the Second World War, tried the German leaders for war crimes, crimes against humanity as well as for crimes against peace. It was composed of one judge and one alternate from each of the four Allied Powers. The Tribunal held its first public meeting in Berlin on 18 October 1945. The trial was begun on 20 November 1945, and continued through 1 October 1946.

[16] Charter of the International Military Tribunal annexed to the London Agreement of 8 August 1945 for the prosecution and punishment of the major war criminals of the European Axis, 82 *UNTS*, p. 279. It was drafted by representatives from the four Allied Powers (the U.S., the U.K., the U.S.S.R. and France).
At its first session, the General Assembly of the United Nations unanimously confirmed the validity of "the principles of international law recognized by the Charter of the Nuremberg Tribunal and the judgment of the Tribunal" by Resolution 95(I) of 11 December, 1946. In 1946, President Harry Truman of the United States had suggested to the General Assembly that the United Nations should reaffirm the principles of the Nuremberg Charter in a Code of Crimes against the peace and Security of Mankind. 75 15 Dep't St. Bull. 954 (24 Nov. 1946). The resolution further requested a new committee to include those principles in an International Criminal Code. In 1950, at its second session, the International Law Commission adopted a formulation of the "Principles of International Law Recognized in the Charter of the Nuremberg Tribunal and in the Judgment of the Tribunal". *YBILC*, Vol. II, pp. 374-378 (1950), document A/1316, paras. 95-127).

[17] After the Nuremberg and Tokyo trials the concept of crimes against peace (including the war of aggression), as defined by the Nuremberg and Tokyo Charters, became part of international law.

[18] For a comprehensive account on the proceedings and outcome of the Conference, *cf.*, *Report of Robert H. Jackson, United States Representative to the International Conference on Military Trials, London, 1945*, Dept. of State Publications, 3080, 1949.

...The following acts, or any of them, are crimes coming within the jurisdiction of the Tribunal for which there shall be individual responsibility:

(a) *Crimes against peace*: Namely, planning, preparation, initiation or waging of a war of aggression, or a war in violation of international treaties, agreements or assurances, or participation in a common plan or conspiracy for the accomplishment of any of the foregoing;[19]

A striking feature of this formulation is that it attempted to define aggression by a mere reference to the element of participation. The underlying idea of the article's scope *ratione materiae* involved the notion of participation, whether active or passive. Such a solution actually evades the issue of definition altogether. Article VI did not include a *definition* of aggression or a war of aggression or what constituted such concepts.[20] The mere mention of "a war of aggression" in paragraph (a) without any indication as to what it means beyond the provision that the planning, preparation, initiation or waging of it, or participation in a common plan or conspiracy for its accomplishment makes it a crime against peace for which there shall be individual responsibility implies that the *definition* of "war of aggression" is to be found in instruments other than the Charter itself.

---

[19] The two other crimes were "War Crimes" (namely, violations of the laws and customs of war), and "Crimes against Humanity" (namely, murder, extermination, enslavement, deportation, and other inhumane acts committed against any civilian). The charge of Crimes Against Peace was a new international criminal concept.

Brownlie found that the provisions on crimes against peace, as finally drafted, were the result of a compromise. The compromise was to make a charge of launching aggressive war alternative or additional to a charge of initiating war in violation of treaties, although if the reference to treaties, agreements, and assurances was a rehearsal of the sources of law then it was tautologous. The result was a clumsy formula which in terms created the distinct offence consisting in violation of international treaties, agreements or assurances. Brownlie, Ian, *International Law and the Use of Force by States*, Oxford, Clarendon Press, 1963, pp. 163f.

[20] Commenting on the issue of the lack of a definition of what constituted an act of aggression in the Charter of the Tribunal, Robert Jackson, Chief Prosecutor for the United States, said that:

"It is perhaps a weakness in this Charter that *it fails itself to define a war of aggression*. Abstractly, the subject is full of difficulty, and all kinds of troublesome hypothetical cases can be conjured up. It is a subject which if the defence should be permitted to go afield beyond the very narrow charge in the indictment, would prolong the trial and involve the Tribunal in insoluble political issues." (Italics added.)
Opening Speeches, 21 November, 1945, p. 40.

Naturally drawing on the Nuremberg Charter, Article 5 on "Jurisdiction over Persons and Offences" of the Charter of the International Military Tribunal for the Far East (Tokyo Tribunal) defined crimes against peace almost identically.[21] The only difference was the addition to the formula copied from Article VI of the Nuremberg Charter of the phrase "declared or undeclared" in respect of a war of aggression. It may have been intended by that addition to emphasize that aggressive war, in whatever disguise, was an international crime. In any case, it was implied in the Charter of Nuremberg.

Based on the logic of the formula arrived at London, the Nuremberg Tribunal proceeded to charge and judge the defendants in a manner that put into effect the link between the Charter (which contained the crimes to be committed by the individual) and aggression (which was to be found elsewhere). It considered that in 1939 aggressive war was already criminalized as a consequence of the Pact for the Renunciation of War, also known as the Kellogg-Briand Pact, signed in Paris on 27 August 1928.[22] The Tribunal referred to the Draft Treaty of Mutual Assistance, the Geneva Protocol, the resolution of the League Assembly of 24 September 1927, and the resolution of the Sixth International Conference of American States declaring aggressive war an international crime.[23] Its conclusion was that:

> All these expressions of opinion, and others that could be cited, so solemnly made, reinforce the construction which the Tribunal placed upon the Pact of Paris, that resort to a war of aggression is not merely illegal, but is criminal. The prohibition of aggressive war demanded by the conscience of the world, finds its expression in the series of pacts and treaties to which the Tribunal has ... referred.[24]

---

[21]   Article 5 read as follows:
"The following acts, or any of them, are crimes coming within the jurisdiction of the Tribunal for which there shall be individual responsibility:
(a) *Crimes against peace*: Namely, the planning, preparation, initiation or waging of a declared or undeclared war of aggression, or a war in violation of international law, treaties, agreements or assurances, or participation in a common plan or conspiracy for the accomplishment of any of the foregoing".

[22]   According to the Pact, war was renounced as an instrument of national policy, and only peaceful means were to be used for the settlement of disputes.

[23]   Brownlie, *op. cit.*, *supra* fn. 19, p. 171.

[24]   Judgment, p. 41. In his dissenting opinion on this very issue in the Trial of Japanese Major War Criminals, Judge Roling of the Netherlands concluded that, although aggressive war was perhaps the subject of moral condemnation, it was "not considered a true crime before and in the beginning of ... [the] war and could not be considered as such for lack of those conditions in international relations on which such a view could be based". Quoted in Brownlie, *op. cit.*, *supra* fn. 19, p. 173.

This distinction between State responsibility and individual responsibility in connection with aggression was recognized and very well preserved in the work of the International Law Commission. Its drafts on State Responsibility[25] and the Code of Crimes against the Peace and Security of Mankind[26] both dealt with the regulation of the "crime of aggression": *the first* as an international crime which gave rise to international responsibility; *the second* as a crime against peace which gave rise to criminal responsibility of individuals. Thus, the rationale of the drafters of the Nuremberg Charter was duly followed by the Commission. The Commission decided not to propose a general definition of crimes against the peace and security of mankind. It took the view that it should rather be left to practice to define the exact contours of the concept of crimes against peace as identified in article VI of the Charter of the Nuremberg Tribunal.[27] The Commission was seeking to define the crime of an individual who, in a case of aggression committed by a State, might be a leader or organizer of the crime and was personally liable for it. It relied on the London formula to prosecute individuals for aggression in the course of its characterization of aggression as an offence against the peace and security of mankind.[28] The drafting of Article 16 of the Code of Offenses Against the Peace and Security of Mankind testifies to this influence. It provides that:

[25] *YBILC*, II, Part Two, 1976, p.118.

[26] Report of the ILC, 6 May-26 July 1996, U.N. GAOR, 51st Sess. Supp. No. 10. U.N. Doc/A51/10. The Commission had considered the draft articles adopted by the Drafting Committee on second reading at its 2437th to 2454th meetings from 6 June to 5 July 1996 and adopted the final text of a set of 20 draft articles constituting the Code.

[27] *YBILC* II, 1996, p. 17.

[28] At the forty-eighth session, the Drafting Committee had continued its work on the basis of two ideas: first, it had taken the view that a clear distinction had to be drawn between the definition of aggression committed by a State, on the one hand, and the crime of aggression committed by an individual on the other. A majority of the members of the Drafting Committee had felt it unnecessary for the Commission to attempt to define aggression, which was covered in the Charter and defined by the General Assembly, especially as individuals, and not States, were the subject of the Code. Summary records of the meetings of the forty-eighth session p. 60.

An individual who, as leader or organizer, actively participates in or orders the planning, preparation, initiation or waging of aggression committed by a State shall be responsible for a crime of aggression.[29]

The phrase "[a]n individual ... shall be responsible for a crime of aggression" indicates that the *scope* of the article is limited to the crime of aggression for the purpose of individual criminal responsibility, where an individual, as leader or organizer, participates in that aggression. At the same time, it refers to "aggression committed by a State". Thus, it does not address the question of the definition of aggression by a State which is beyond the scope of the Code, and, therefore, leaving it for a different set of rules of international law.[30]

Clearly, the formula establishing the legal nexus between aggression and the act of the individual implicated in it, has been followed for more than fifty years. That solution *is* in our view the only legally sound one to which the PrepCom of the ICC and the Assembly of States Parties should have recourse.

In order to prove the validity of this "formula" on the theoretical and practical levels, let us address the two components which give it effect, namely, the role of the individual in aggression and *a* definition of aggression.

The Individual and the Crime of Aggression

Although it is not settled whether the *criminal responsibility* of States has been sufficiently elaborated in generally recognized international norms so as to be suitable for application by way of positive international law, it is established law that an internationally wrongful act that *could* be perpetrated by an individual may be attributed to the State,[31] and, thus,

---

[29] "Leaders" or "organizers", an expression that was taken from the Charter of the Nuremberg Tribunal, must be understood in the broad sense, that is to say, as referring, in addition to the members of a Government, to persons occupying high-level posts in the military, the diplomatic corps, political parties and industry, as recognized by the Nuremberg Tribunal that: "Hitler could not make aggressive war by himself. He had to have the cooperation of statesmen, military leaders, diplomats and businessmen". *YBILC* II, 1996, p. 43. Simple soldiers, who for reasons of policy, ought in the case of aggression to be exempt from responsibility.

[30] The internationally agreed definition of aggression was only reached in 1974 in the General Assembly of the United Nations.

[31] This is with due regard to the rules on attribution of wrongful acts to the State reflected in Articles 8, 9 and 10 of the Draft Articles on State Responsibility of the ILC. Imputation must, of course, be distinguished from responsibility.

engage its international responsibility. In fact, the attribution of a wrongful act to a State is the attribution of a conduct by the individual to that State. This logic cannot, however, apply to the *sui generis* situation of aggression as it (i.e., aggression) presupposes the reverse sequence of this order. The Charter-based act of aggression can only, *ratione personae*, be committed by a State and not an individual.[32] And, as a result, the international responsibility of the State is engaged *ab initio* regardless of the question of individual responsibility. How could it be expected in the case of aggression that individual responsibility be established first without a prior determination of the wrong-doing on the part of the State? Whence, what is needed for the purposes of criminal prosecution of an individual is the attribution to that individual of the wrongful acts resulting in or leading to the aggression. This *inevitable* link between the international responsibility of the State for aggression and individual criminal responsibility requires a determination on the *commission* of aggression, *ratione materiae*. Only after a State has been declared as an aggressor (pursuant to the Charter of United Nations and the definition of aggression annexed to General Assembly resolution 3314), may an individual – for the purposes of individual criminal responsibility, and more particularly the Statute of the ICC – be tried on the basis of that legal nexus.

As earlier explained, under the so-called *definition of aggression* in the Charter of the Nuremberg Tribunal and, subsequently, in the Charter of the Tokyo Tribunal, individual involvement was limited to that of a leader or organizer.[33] Thus, the focus was on the identification of the *role* of an individual in the commission of aggression by a State. This continued into the present, but became even more emphasized and clarified. Article 16 of the draft Code of Offenses Against the Peace and Security of Mankind referred to "aggression committed by a State" as an indication that the commission of aggression is a *sine qua non* condition for the attribution to

---

[32] Traditionally it is called a State-crime as the State was the only actor on the international level before new actors were introduced in international relations and international law. In its resolution 405 (1977) of 14 April 1977, the Security Council had used the word "aggression", without designating any State, in connection with the case of the mercenaries who had attacked Benin in 1977. No State was identified because some Council Members, some of them with veto powers, had wanted it that way. It is true that the question of transboundary attacks by non-governmental groups had not been discussed by the ILC. However, it would be a mistake to view those transboundary crimes, attacks or acts of violence perpetrated by non-governmental groups as being covered only by ordinary criminal law.

[33] The Charter and the Judgment of the Nuremberg Tribunal are the main sources of authority with regard to individual criminal responsibility for acts of aggression. *Cf., YBILC* II, 1996, p. 43.

an individual of responsibility for a crime of aggression. The wording of Article 16 of the Code of Offenses Against the Peace and Security of Mankind covered all categories of individuals who would be made criminally responsible for the crime of aggression at the political, military, financial, economic or any other level. So far as the scope *ratione personae* is concerned, the chain of responsibility in the case of aggression committed by a State naturally lay at the highest level in the political and military structure of the State or in its economic and financial life. The article further provided that an individual, as leader or organizer, participates in that aggression.[34] It is this *participation* that the article defined as a crime against the peace and security of mankind.[35] It thus reaffirmed the criminal responsibility of the participants in a crime of aggression.

True, only the State is capable of committing aggression, but it is an abstract entity which inevitably requires action by the individuals who plan and others who execute.[36] In this respect, the Nuremberg Tribunal stated that:

> Crimes against international law are committed by men, not by abstract entities, and only by punishing individuals who commit such crimes can the provisions of international law be enforced.[37]

In order to close the circle, there remains to ensure that the principle of *nullum crimen sine lege* is safeguarded. There have to be definite criteria against which the accused may take his decisions and plan his actions. What then is "aggression" to which reference should be made in order to hold individuals accountable? What is its definition? And what is its value?

---

[34] It restricted responsibility for a crime of aggression to the category of leaders or organizers, but listed a wide range of activities that would make such individuals responsible for the crime.

[35] The crime of aggression by an individual must involve participation in the activity of the State at a policy-making level in order to ensure the presence of the element of *mens rea*.

[36] The International Law Commission noted that "A State can commit aggression only with the active participation of the individuals who have the necessary authority or power to plan, prepare, initiate or wage aggression." Report of the ILC, 6 May–26 July 1996, U.N. GAOR, 51st Sess. Supp. No. 10. U.N. Doc. A/51/10, p. 84.

[37] Judgment, p. 220.

Defining Aggression: the Road to the General Assembly Resolution 3314 (XXIX)

The only authoritative and universally agreed definition of aggression is annexed to General Assembly resolution 3314 (XXIX) adopted on 14 December 1974. The road to that definition was a long and difficult one. The road to the adoption of resolution 3314 was a long and strenuous one which may be traced back to the days of the League of Nations.

The first systematic efforts to define aggression came with the advent of the League of Nations.[38] According to the Covenant, the members of the League undertook to "preserve as against external aggression the territorial integrity and existing political independence of all the members of the organization".[39] The Covenant did not, however, contain any definition of aggression.[40] The criteria for determining whether aggression had occurred was debated at length; but to no avail. Every nation could decide for itself whether the "aggression" was adequate to trigger economic sanctions. An Advisory Committee of Jurists, appointed by the League of Nations, recommended the establishment of a High Court competent to prosecute crimes committed against International public order or against the universal law of nations. The court would define the nature of the crimes to be tried, fix penalties, decide the appropriate means of carrying out the sentences and formulate its own rules of procedure. Upon receipt of the recommendation of the jurists, the Legal Committee of the League reported that:

> There is not yet any international penal law recognized by all nations, and that if it were possible to refer certain crimes to any jurisdiction it would be more practical to establish a special chamber of the Permanent Court of International Justice.

In 1922 resolution 14 proposed the creation of a Treaty of Mutual Guarantee, and a Temporary Mixed Commission was assigned to prepare such a treaty. The draft Treaty spoke of aggressive war and aggression

---

[38]   The League had also sponsored a number of treaties in which aggression was specifically prohibited. Stone, Julius, *Aggression and World Order*, Berkeley, University of California Press, 1958, p. 29.

[39]   Article 10.

[40]   It has to be remembered that war was not completely outlawed. Resort to war would only subject its perpetrators to the risk of economic sanctions as well as expulsion from the League and military force. Article 16.

without defining what was meant by these terms. This effort was also not successful and was terminated by 1923.[41] The whole issue was deferred by the League of Nations at the end of the 1920s. The Assembly of the League declared, on 24 September 1927, that a war of aggression was "an international crime".

On 6 February 1933, the Soviet Union submitted the first definition of aggression to the General Commission of the Disarmament Conference.[42] It was based on the principle of *priority* in declaring that the aggressor in an international conflict shall be considered that State which is the first to take certain actions. This effort failed to gain general acceptance by the end of the Conference in 1934.[43]

Thus, the early attempts to define aggression in the days of the League did not come to fruition.[44]

Albeit the many attempts made to define aggression before the Second World War, it is only after the Charter of the Nuremberg Tribunal that the definition of aggression has undergone significant development until the adoption of resolution 3314 of 1974. In fact, in resolution 2330 (XXII) of 18 December 1967 entitled "Need to expedite the drafting of a definition of aggression in the light of the present international situation",[45] the General Assembly of the United Nations noted that "there was still at that date [in 1967] *no generally recognized* definition of aggression",[46] thus confirming that the definition contained in Principle VI of the Charter of Nuremberg was not *in itself* conceived as a "definition of aggression", and that one was yet to be arrived at.

But how did the Assembly arrive at that conclusion in 1967? What happened some twenty years earlier was that the question was considered by the San Francisco Conference in 1945, but to no avail. Countries from the Third World attending the Conference, such as Egypt and Iran, supported the idea of incorporating a definition of aggression into the Charter when the question of aggression was considered by the Third

---

[41]   Broms, Bengt, The Definition of Aggression, *RCADI*, 1977-I Vol. 154, p. 306.

[42]   This definition was referred to as the Litvinov-Politis definition.

[43]   Broms, *op. cit.*, p. 309.

[44]   For a detailed history of the question of defining aggression in the era of the League, *cf.*, Official Records of the General Assembly, Seventh Session, Annexes, agenda item 54, document A /2211.

[45]   The resolution was drafted and presented by Algeria, Burma, Cameroon, Cyprus, Ghana, Guinea, India, Indonesia, Jordan, Kenya, Kuwait, Lebanon, Liberia, Malaysia, Mauritania, Morocco, Nigeria, Romania, Sudan, Syria, United Arab Republic, United Republic of Tanzania, Yemen, Yugoslavia, and Zambia. Doc. A/C.6/L.644.

[46]   Italics added.

Committee of the Third Commission.[47] Others, such as the Philippines and Bolivia, presented draft definitions in that connection.[48] The Committee discussed both proposals at length. However, it was finally decided by the Conference not to introduce a definition into the Charter which was signed on 26 June 1945. It was hoped at that point that the Security Council would "determine the existence of any threat to the peace, breach of the peace, or act of aggression" pursuant to Article 39 of the Charter. Thus, this serious attempt was not successful in reaching a final result. However, this endeavor proved useful in the following years as it created wide awareness of the definition of aggression. It also served as a catalyst for the following attempts.

Later, in 1950 the Security Council was confronted with the first case of aggression – and the only one that the Council pronounced itself on (and not explicitly) for more than 45 years before it did so very willingly and discriminately in the 1990s – namely, the Korean crisis resulting from the invasion by the armed forces of the People's Republic of Korea of the territory of South Korea. Yugoslavia, in connection with the Agenda item entitled "Duties of States in the Event of the Outbreak of Hostilities", pioneered in directing the attention of the General Assembly to the question of defining aggression. It developed this proposal further during the general debate.[49] Due to the problems confronted by the Security Council in that instance, the Soviet Union (which was absent from the Council from 10 January to 1 August, 1950, because of its position on the question of the representation of China in the United Nations) submitted on 4 November, 1950, a proposal in connection with the definition of aggression containing a list of acts to be considered aggressive as it had done in 1933.[50] An important *procedural* move by Syria followed. It submitted a draft resolution to the First Committee on the referral of the problem of defining aggression to the International Law Commission. And so, by resolution 378

---

[47] *Cf.*, Broms, *op. cit.*, pp. 315 f.; and Rifaat, Ahmed, *International Aggression: A Study of the Legal Concept: Its Development and Definition in International Law*, Stockholm, Almquvist & Wiksell International, 1979, p. 108. For views against the inclusion of a definition in the Charter see the position of New Zealand reproduced in Rifaat, *ibid.*, pp. 108 f. The United Kingdom and Denmark also were among those opposing defining aggression.

[48] *Documents of the United Nations Conference on International Organization*, San Francisco, 1945, Vol. III, p. 538 and p. 585 respectively. These proposals were supported by Colombia, Egypt, Ethiopia, Guatemala, Honduras, Iran, Mexico, and Uruguay.

[49] For the details of this proposal *cf.*, Broms, *op. cit.*, pp. 316 f.

[50] *Official Records of the General Assembly, Fifth Session*, Annexes, Agenda Item 72, Doc. A/C. 1/608, 1950, pp. 4 f.

B (V) of 17 November, 1950,[51] the General Assembly referred the proposal to the International Law Commission.[52] After deliberating over the definition of aggression in connection with its work on the Draft Code of Offences against the Peace and Security of Mankind which it was undertaking at that time,[53] the Commission decided that aggression should *not* be defined and refused to resume work on it.[54] The matter came back to the General Assembly. From that date onwards the General Assembly engaged in the exercise to define aggression, and established successive special committees to that end.

Delegations in the Sixth Committee, in particular from Bolivia, Egypt, Iran, Iraq, Lebanon, Mexico, Panama, Paraguay, Peru, Syria and Yemen, were very determined to arrive at a definition and were a driving force in the establishment of the several committees entrusted with defining aggression notwithstanding the repeated attempts by the United States and its allies, particularly the United Kingdom, to put off the whole exercise of defining aggression altogether.[55] Consequently, the first Special Committee on the Question of Defining Aggression was set up by General Assembly

---

[51] The Syrian draft was replaced by another co-sponsored jointly by Syria and Bolivia (A/C.1/625).

[52] *Cf.*, *Official Records of the General Assembly, Fifth Session, First Committee*, 387th meeting, para. 42. For the work of the Commission see *Report of the International Law Commission* on its third session, 16 May-27 July, 1951, pp. 8-10. Broms explains that there were no guidelines as to the definition of aggression in this resolution except that the Soviet proposal and all the records of the First Committee were referred to the International Law Commission which was asked to formulate its conclusions as soon as possible. *Op. cit.*, p. 318.

[53] The Draft Code of Offences against Peace and Security of Mankind was finalized in 1951 and adopted by the Sixth Committee in 1954. The General Assembly, by its resolution 177 (II) of 21 November 1947, had directed the Commission to: (a) formulate the principles of international law recognized in the Charter of the Nuremberg Tribunal and in the Judgment of the Tribunal; and (b) prepare a draft code of offences against the peace and security of mankind, indicating clearly the place to be accorded to the principles mentioned in (a) above.

[54] The Commission rejected the draft definition it was considering by a roll-call of 7 against 3. Furthermore, a proposal to continue working on the definition was rejected by 6 votes to 4. However, the Commission satisfied itself by including in Article 2 of the Draft Code the following:
"The following acts are offences against the peace and security of mankind:
(1) Any act of aggression, including the employment by the authorities of a State of armed force against another State for any purpose other than national or collective self-defence or in pursuance of a decision or recommendation by a competent organ of the United Nations.
(2) Any threat by the authorities of a State to resort to an act of aggression against another State. ...."

[55] The United States representative had requested in 1956 the General assembly to postpone its work on the definition of aggression *indefinitely*. On the position of the United States and the United Kingdom and others, *cf.*, Broms, *op. cit.*, in particular, pp. 320-35.

resolution 688 (VII) of 20 December, 1952. It was composed of fifteen members. It lasted from 1953 to 1954.[56] The second Special Committee established in accordance with resolution 895 (IX) of 4 December, 1954, remained in force between 1956 and 1957.[57] This Committee consisted of nineteen members. The third one, consisting of twenty one members, was established under resolution 1181 (XII) of 29 November, 1957, and continued from 1959 to 1967.[58] Despite such numerous efforts no definition was approved.

Finally, in 1967, pursuant to resolution 2330 (XXII) referred to above, the Assembly established yet a fourth, but last, Special Committee on the Question of Defining Aggression. That one was successful in drafting the definition annexed to General Assembly resolution 3314 of 14 December, 1974.[59] It is at that date in 1974 that the Assembly satisfied its need to arrive at what it had called seven years earlier a "generally recognized definition of aggression". This is the critical date which should be referred to in determining an *agreed* definition of aggression.

The work of the Special Committee, and especially the role of the Third World delegations deserves attention. The Committee, which held its first meeting in Geneva on 4 June, 1968, had before it five draft proposals. All of them, except for a procedural one presented by the Soviet Union on the future work of the Committee,[60] came from Third World countries.[61]

---

[56] Report of Special Committee, 1953, U. N. Doc. A/2638, Aug. 24-Sept. 21, 1953.

[57] Report of Special Committee, 1956, U.N. Doc. A/3574, Nov. 27, 1957.

[58] Report of Special Committee, 1959, U.N. Doc. A/AC.91/2, April 24, 1959; Doc. A/AC.91/3, 9 April, 1962; and Doc. A/AC.91/5, 16 April, 1965.

[59] Pursuant to paragraph 2 of resolution 2330 (XXII), the President of the General Assembly appointed the following thirty-five Member States to serve on the Special Committee: Algeria, Australia, Bulgaria, Canada, Colombia, Congo (Democratic Republic of), Cyprus, Czechoslovakia, Ecuador, Finland, France, Ghana, Guyana, Haiti, Indonesia, Iran, Iraq, Italy, Japan, Madagascar, Mexico, Norway, Romania, Sierra Leone, Spain, Sudan, Syria, Turkey, Uganda, Union of Soviet Socialist Republics, United Arab Republic, United Kingdom of Great Britain and Northern Ireland, United States of America, Uruguay and Yugoslavia.Doc. A/7061. The Committee elected Mustafa Kamil Yasseen, an eminent Iraqi jurist, as its Chairman.

[60] A/AC.134/L.7, 5 July 1968.

[61] The four proposals were presented by the following States successively: Algeria, the Congo (Democratic Republic of), Cyprus, Ghana, Guyana, Indonesia. Madagascar, Sudan, Syria, Uganda, the United Arab Republic and Yugoslavia (A/AC.134/L.3 and Corr.1 and 2 and Add.1, 25 June 1968); Colombia, Ecuador, Mexico and Uruguay (A/AC.134/L.4/Rev.1 and Corr. 1 and Add.1, 26 June 1968); Colombia, Congo (Democratic Republic of), Cyprus, Ecuador, Ghana, Guyana, Indonesia, Iran, Mexico, Spain, Uganda, Uruguay and Yugoslavia (A/AC.134/L.6 and Add.1 and 2, 3 July 1968); Sudan and the United Arab Republic (A/AC.134/L.8, 6 July 1968).

Those proposals enjoyed wide appreciation by other members of the Committee and were considered a veritable contribution towards the completion of its task.[62] They were the bases for discussions, future proposals and counter-proposals.[63]

During the deliberations of the Special Committee, three types of definitions were discussed: a general or generic definition based on a *deductive* approach, an enumerative definition based on an *inductive* approach in which a list of acts constituting aggression in a non-exhaustive manner appears, and a combined or composite one.[64] This latter type was the one on which the Special Committee settled.

The Sixth Committee adopted the text of the draft consolidated definition of aggression by consensus,[65] and recommended that the General Assembly adopt the definition, which it did on 14 December 1974, without a vote.

The Legal Content and Customary Nature of the Definition of Aggression

The "Definition of Aggression" annexed to resolution 3314 (XXIX) of 1974 employed two approaches at the same time: a *deductive* approach in Article 1 in which it proposed a general formula,[66] and an *inductive* approach in which it enumerated acts which constitute aggression in a non-

---

[62]   *Cf.*, *Official Records of the General Assembly, Twenty-third Session*, Agenda item 86, Doc. A/7185/Rev.1, paragraph 67.

[63]   E.g. the draft of the Union of Soviet Socialist Republics (A/AC.134/L.12); the new Thirteen-Power draft submitted by Colombia, Cyprus, Ecuador, Ghana, Guyana, Haiti, Iran, Madagascar, Mexico, Spain, Uganda, Uruguay and Yugoslavia (A/AC.134/L.16 and Add.1 and 2); and the Six-Power draft by Australia, Canada, Italy, Japan, United Kingdom of Great Britain and Northern Ireland and the United States of America (A/AC.134/L.17 and Add.1).

[64]   Egypt, France, Iraq and Yugoslavia were in favour of a combined definition of aggression, i.e., a combination between the general and enumerative types of definition, see *Official Records of the General Assembly, Seventh Session*, Annexes, Agenda item 54, Doc. A/2162 and Add. I, pp. 2 ff.

[65]   *Cf.*, Report of the Sixth Committee, GAOR, 29th session, Annexes, Agenda Item 86 (A/9890), 1974. The Committee considered the matter between 8 October and 22 November 1974.

[66]   Article 1 reads:
"Aggression is the use of armed force by a State against the sovereignty, territorial integrity or political independence of another State, or in any other manner inconsistent with the Charter of the United Nations, as set out in this Definition."

exhaustive manner as appears in Article 3.[67] Resolution 3314 deals with aggression by States, not with the crimes of individuals. As such, and without the appropriate *cross-reference* to the act of the individual it is of no use whatsoever for the purposes of criminal law.

As to the significance and value of the Definition of Aggression annexed to resolution 3314, it has been argued by some delegations in the PrepCom that the International Court of Justice – in its Judgement in 1986 in the case concerning *Military and Paramilitary Activities in and against Nicaragua*,[68] – did not consider that definition, and in particular Article 3, as reflective of customary international law. The reason behind such a suggestion – it was contended – was that the Court explicitly singled out sub-paragraph (*g*) of Article 3 as a reflection of such custom.[69] Although this is true, it does not represent the entire truth.

Sub-paragraph (*g*) – the last of the sub-paragraphs of Article 3 in terms of order and the last to be negotiated in the Special Committee – happened to be one of the most problematic provisions in the Committee. When in the course of the consideration by the World Court of whether the sending by or on behalf of a State of armed bands, groups, irregulars or mercenaries which carry out acts of armed force against another State, amounted to aggression, the Court relied on sub-paragraph (*g*) to prove that

---

[67] Article 3 stipulates that:

"Any of the following acts, regardless of a declaration of war, shall, subject to and in accordance with the provisions of article 2, qualify as an act of aggression:

(a) The invasion or attack by the armed forces of a State of the territory of another State or any military occupation, however temporary, resulting from such invasion or attack, or any annexation by the use of force of the territory of another State or part thereof;

(b) Bombardment by the armed forces of a State against the territory of another State or the use of any weapons by a State against the territory of another State;

(c) The blockade of the ports or coasts of a State by the armed forces of another State;

(d) An attack by the armed forces of a State on the land, sea or air forces, or marine and air fleets of another State;

(e) The use of armed forces of one State which are within the territory of another State with the agreement of the receiving State, in contravention of the conditions provided for in the agreement or any extension of their presence in such territory beyond the termination of the agreement;

(f) The action of a State in allowing its territory, which it has placed at the disposal of another State, to be used by that other State for perpetrating an act of aggression against a third State;

(g) The sending by or on behalf of a State of armed bands, groups, irregulars or mercenaries, which carry out acts of armed force against another State of such gravity as to amount to the acts listed above, or its substantial involvement therein."

[68] *Military and Paramilitary Activities in and against Nicaragua (Nicaragua* v. *United States of America), Merits, Judgment of 27 June 1986, I.C.J. Reports 1986*, p. 14.

[69] *Ibid.*, para. 195 at p. 103.

it actually so amounted. In the view of the Court, the rule contained in sub-paragraph (*g*) was already in 1986 of a customary value. Thus, the Court intended to emphasize the customary nature of the provision in that sub-paragraph as it was aware of its legislative background. This was not to say that only that sub-paragraph reflected custom. What is important here, is that no logic may suggest that what was a most problematic provision would become customary law, while others which were universally accepted (as they were Charter-based) were not. In fact, the Court, by referring to that particular sub-paragraph wanted to say that it had the same status as the others which were already reflective of custom.

Other delegations in the Prep Com, and particularly the representatives of the five permanent members of the Security Council, basing themselves probably on the penultimate preambular paragraph of resolution 3314, maintain that the Definition of Aggression was only to serve as a guidance for the determination of acts of aggression by the Security Council. We cannot share this restrictive interpretation; the resolution should be read integrally. Its fourth preambular paragraph clearly, and unambiguously, refers to the powers and functions of organs of the United Nations, which is to say that other organs may also be involved in the question of aggression. The practice of the General Assembly and the International Court of Justice supports this understanding as will be discussed further below.

Hence, no definition exists for aggression other than the one contained in General Assembly resolution 3314 (XXIX).

The Relationship between the ICC and the Security Council

The relationship between the Court and the Security Council has probably caused more controversy and consumed more time than any other issue related to the Statute. In general, that relationship is regulated by articles 5(2), 13(b) and 16 of the Statute of the ICC. However, the relationship between the ICC and the Council with respect to aggression is regulated by Article 5. Although paragraph 2 of that article does not make explicit reference to the Security Council,[70] the provision that the exercise of the Court of its jurisdiction with respect to the crime of aggression shall "be consistent with the relevant provision of the Charter of the United Nations" implies the involvement of the Security Council; but not exclusively.

There is no ambiguity in that the Charter of the United Nations entrusts the Security Council with the task of determining the existence of any act of aggression in accordance with Articles 39 and 24. As a political and executive body it is expected to do that. However, any such determination by the Council will not be without legal effects (whether positive or negative) on the ICC. If, for example, the Council declares a case of aggression the Court will be able to exercise its jurisdiction over this crime. But a finding by the Court that there was no legal nexus between a situation of aggression determined by the Council and the act of the individuals alleged to be implicated in it will undoubtedly put in question that determination, thus putting the ICC in direct conflict with the Security Council. On the other hand if the Council failed – for whatever reasons – to make a determination that there existed an act of aggression,[71] the ICC would not be able to exercise its jurisdiction with respect to aggression if the Council were to be the only body allowed to make such determinations.[72]

As to the *exclusive* powers of the Security Council in this respect, some members of the PrepCom argue that absent an initial determination by it, the Court should only have the right to investigate other crimes within its jurisdiction in an attempt to cover the same acts that the Council would have otherwise declared as aggression. If one were to submit to this view, he would, in fact, be washing-out the provisions on aggression from the Statute, which is unthinkable after so many decades since the inclusion of that crime in the Nuremberg and Tokyo Charters. Both in law and in fact, the Council's inability to fulfill its duties – due to the inherent deficiencies

---

[70] This is a significant departure from the Article 23 of the ILC draft which made plain that no complaint of aggression could be brought unless the Security Council determined first that a State had committed the act of aggression which was the subject of the complaint. Article 23(2) stipulated that it would be necessary "to ensure that prosecutions are brought for aggression only if the Security Council first determines that the state in question has committed aggression". Report of the International Law Commission on the work of its Forty-sixth Session, 2 May-22 July 1994, U.N. GAOR, 49th Sess., Supp. No. 10, U.N. Doc. A/49/10, at 72.

[71] For instance, in connection with the Suez crisis in which Member States of the United Nations were called upon to assist the Security Council under Article 42 of the Charter to "halt the aggression", France and the United Kingdom used their right of veto to block the resolution.

[72] The same legal effect would possibly ensue from a determination by any other political body.

of the Charter and the over-politicisation of the Council – does not prevent other organs from acting in cases relating to the maintenance of international peace and security. For example, General Assembly resolution 377 of 1950, also known as the "Uniting for Peace" resolution, has enabled the General Assembly to intervene eight times in cases where the Council's ability to exercise its *primary* responsibility for the maintenance of international peace and security was blocked. Equally, the International Court of Justice – in the *Nicaragua* case cited above – had to make its own determination of acts of aggression to determine whether the Respondent (the United States) had a right to self-defense in response to certain actions taken by the Applicant (Nicaragua).

There is no reason why the International Criminal Court should be impeded if the Security Council was blocked from fulfilling its Charter-based duties. The Council's inability to react to cases of aggression most of the time is not fictitious. From the day of its inception up to 1990, and despite all the atrocities and acts of sheer aggression that the world had witnessed, the Council had only in one single instance declared that there was a case of aggression. That was the Korean case, referred to above, which was taught to students of international law and international relations as the only existing species of aggression determined by the Council. Even after the events which had erupted in the Persian Gulf in the beginning of the 1990s the Council has acted selectively in determining cases of aggression. In consequence, aggressors survived their evil.

Conclusions

Aggression *per se* is a crime that, unlike all the others covered by the Statute, is committed by a collectivity and not by an individual, who alone falls under the jurisdiction *ratione personae* of the ICC. And, as such, the Court cannot exercise its jurisdiction over it *directly*. As a result, the Statute-based condition of preparing a provision defining the crime of aggression does not depend on drafting a *definition* of aggression in the literal meaning of the term. Rather, it requires a formulation in which the *role* or *involvement* of the individual in the commission of "aggression" (which is *already* defined) could be identified for the purposes of attributing a criminal act to an individual.

As for the determination of situations of aggression, two findings have to be recalled. First, the Security Council is not the sole authority vested with powers in this respect. It is practically and legally possible for the General Assembly of the United Nations and the International Court of Justice to make such determinations.

Second, the conditions of the exercise of the ICC of its jurisdiction over the crime of aggression, in terms of the relationship between it and the Security Council with respect to that crime, have been made difficult as a result of the fact that at the time of constructing the Charter design the international judicial system did not include a permanent international criminal instance. Thus, the drafting of the wide and powerful prerogatives of the Council did not necessarily foresee the role of other future institutions such as the ICC. Accordingly, the concern over the possible incompatibility between the Statute of the ICC and the Charter has contributed to the delay in an agreement on the provisions on the crime of aggression. The negotiators at the PrepCom and the Diplomatic Conference at Rome were quite aware that while the determination by the Council of a situation of aggression was a political decision, the ICC was required to analyse the situation by applying a totally different analytical tool: the judicial process. This difference in the gauging systems of the Court and the Security Council is likely to lead to different findings. Whence, any sound solution to the question of the relationship between the ICC and the Council will depend primarily on how it eliminates the possibility of inconsistency between the decisions of the two institutions. Of course, this has to be with full respect to the independence of the ICC so that it may fulfill its role in the delivery of international justice.

6. Aggression and the ICC: Views on Certain Ideas and their Potential for a Solution

PHANI DASCALOPOULOU-LIVADA*

If the establishment of the ICC can be pictured as the conquest of the West, then aggression is the last frontier. Once this is conquered, too, then the achievement is complete. I feel that this frontier should be reached, because, apart from anything else, we are under a historical duty to do so.

Still, the harsh reality remains that the work of the PrepCom on this question has remained slow despite the fact that we have moved from sterile political statements and confrontation to in-depth discussions of the problems involved. As the time of waiting until the establishment of the ICC *corpore* tends to become shorter and shorter – belying the Cassandras across the spectrum who would have us believe that the waiting period would be lost from our eyesight into the distant future –, it is now reasonable to expect that the Court will be there in a year's time or so. This makes the work on aggression urgent and pressing. It is not, any more, a matter of settling other matters first and then we shall see. It is rather a question of having the matter settled now, within the coming months, so that we first do our duty as to the mandate entrusted to the PrepCom by the Rome Conference and second and most important that we settle a matter which is of undeniable importance.

Of course even discussing a settlement shows how far removed we are from the beginning of the ICC enterprise. I can remember, at those early times of the *ad hoc* Committee on the ICC, the various arguments which were heard against including aggression in the jurisdiction of the ICC. They ranged from the technical and legal to the political. Most prominent among the latter was the argument that "it will not succeed", and maybe it will lead

---

* Legal Adviser, Head of the Section of Public International Law, Legal Department, Ministry of Foreign Affairs, Athens, Greece.

the whole project to disaster – an argument which was put forward even by staunch supporters of the ICC. Even the NGOs, usually so eloquent pressing on all other matters, were surprisingly silent on this question which is certainly much more important than any single individual crime in the Statute. The explanation was the same: fear, fear of collapse of the whole effort, fear to deal with a matter which was considered too political, too difficult, too beyond our powers and means, in a nutshell too much of a taboo. Still, few at first, many more later – dreamers, risk-takers, those who had taken the lessons of history to heart or those who knew first-hand what aggression was all about –, refused to succumb to that fear. And they were rewarded – at least partially – on both counts, since the Statute is there and its jurisdiction already includes aggression, while more and more states come forward in favor of finding a meaningful solution to our current problems because, if we do not, they realize that a great deal of the importance of the Statute to them will not be there.

This brings me back to the actual reality of the situation and to the real problems we are faced with. As we all know very well, these problems are the question of the definition and, to cut a long story short, the question of the relationship between the ICC and the Security Council on the question of aggression.

Of course, both questions are closely connected and, as a consequence, they can hardly be separated. However, I could, I believe, isolate certain matters relating to the definition *stricto sensu* and express some views on them. Let me first say epigrammatically that on the question of the definition, as much as it can be considered distinct from the other ones or one, it would seem that the problems are not insurmountable. First of all, I believe that the problem of choosing between a generic and an enumerative approach is clearly overstated. I have always been among those who believed that a generic approach is better, for the very practical reason that it would present better chances to succeed in rallying consensus. Resolution 3314, on the other hand, would continue to be very relevant, since the Court would inexorably resort to it when dealing with a specific case which has been brought before it. A generic definition would simply spare us the rancours of having to decide on each one of the specific cases mentioned, illustratively, we should not forget, by that Resolution and, further on, of perhaps including other cases which could certainly be important to some. It would also avoid the potential danger of reopening questions which had caused a lot of strife in the discussions of Resolution 3314. Still, the fact cannot be ignored that a considerable number of delegations insist that the list of 3314 should be included in the definition. Although there should not be any theoretical objection to this approach, the proposals on the table which espouse it – e.g. the Egyptian-Italian proposal – appealing as they are by the mere repetition of such a remarkable achievement as Resolution 3314 undoubtedly is, fail to respond, by conveniently leaving both options open, to the principal problem of whether the list is going to be restrictive or illustrative. If it is going to be restrictive, then we depart from the 3314 precedent. Furthermore, and surely more importantly, a restrictive character of the list would open the way for the inclusion of further cases and a general reopening of the questions which had been so extensively discussed – and certainly not always or not always successfully resolved – in connection with Resolution 3314. If, on the other hand, the illustrative character of the cases cited in that Resolution is kept, it is certain that the question of the applicability of the principle of legality will be raised.

Another matter is the substantial question of the threshold to be used, or the extent to which aggression will be covered under either the generic or the enumerative approach, although the question becomes much more acute in the former case. During the Rome Conference we briefly dealt with this question in the context of the generic approach. At the centre of discussions was a proposal – based on a German idea – which was tabled as a package. However, the problem was never resolved. The same idea is still under consideration by the PrepCom. In its substance, the proposal purports to restrict the definition of aggression by excluding from it anything which goes beyond occupation or annexation or the intention thereof. However, states seem not to be willing to consider that those responsible for acts which, although not amounting to occupation or annexation or having the object of either of those, undoubtedly constitute aggression, should not be subjected to the jurisdiction of the Court.

Another idea which has the same restricting effect as the proposal described above has been advocated by the United Kingdom and is also contained in a proposal by Russia. By employing the phrase "war of aggression" instead of "aggression" these suggestions purport to limit the jurisdiction of the ICC to full-fledged war alone. Under such a proposal, if I interpret correctly the thoughts of its proponents, cases such as that of "humanitarian intervention" would be left out of the jurisdictional reach of the Court. It has been argued, in support of this idea, that the only precedent as far as attributing criminal responsibility to individuals for aggression is concerned, has been in the context of the Nuremberg and Tokyo trials, and in those, the applicable law spoke only of "war of aggression". The international crime, that is, can only be the war of aggression, not aggression pure and simple.

We would not, perhaps, have the time to go into the merits of this suggestion. I will therefore just comment on the terminological question and the supposed *"bagage juridique"* that it carries. In my view, up to now the words «war of aggression» and "aggression" seem to have been rather indiscriminately used in the relevant texts. Thus, article 6 of the Nuremberg Charter and article 5 of the Charter of the Tokyo Tribunal refer to "war of aggression" as does the Control Council for Germany Law No. 10. Conversely, neither General Assembly Resolution 3314 (with the sole exception of art. 5(2)), nor the draft Code of crimes against the peace and security of mankind speak of war of aggression but only of aggression, to which they attribute the gravest consequences.

Looking more closely into the definitions of those texts, it is perhaps interesting to see the different nuances employed. Thus, the Nuremberg Charter defines as "crimes against peace" – the terminology of the times for aggression – as "planning, preparation, initiation or waging a war of aggression, or a war in violation of international Treaties, agreements or assurances, or participation in a common plan or conspiracy for the accomplishment of any of the foregoing".

The Charter of the International Military Tribunal for the Far East also contained a similar definition in its article 5.

The surprise comes from the Allied Control Council Law No. 10 of December 20, 1945, which formed the basis of the trials against special groups of accused. Article II, para. 1(a) of Law No. 10 defines crimes against peace as follows:

> Initiation of invasions of other countries and wars of aggression in violation of international laws and treaties, including but not limited to planning, preparation, initiation or waging a war of aggression, or a war in violation of international treaties, agreements or assurances, or participation in a common plan or conspiracy for the accomplishment of any of the above.[1]

This last definition makes clear that even in Nuremberg the crime of aggression was not perceived only as "a war of aggression". The phrase "initiation of invasions of other countries" in Control Council Law no. 10 clearly encompasses not only full war but also its lesser manifestations,

---

[1]   On that basis judgments were delivered in connection with crimes against peace in the *I.G. Farben* case (Case 6), the *Krupp* case (case 10), *Greselt* case (Case 8), *Foreign Office* case (Case 11) and *High Command* case (Case 12).

which are described as "initiation of invasions of other countries". As there is no reason why there should be any differentiation between this law and the other instruments which were applied in the Nuremberg trials, it can be concluded that the words "war of aggression" and "aggression" are used alternatively and indiscriminately. The legal doctrine seems to corroborate this view, and I will just refer to B.B. Ferencz who, referring to the discussion of the definition of aggression in Resolution 3314 art. 2 notes that the insertion of the word "war" there "raised the problem of who was to decide whether or not a state of war existed and seemed to make a distinction between aggression and aggressive war, despite the fact that no such distinction had appeared in the Nuremberg principles or in the discussions of the International Law Association or the UN General Assembly".[2]

Despite the fact that the application of the notion of "war of aggression" seems to be neither workable nor desirable, we have to admit that there is a need for some qualifier so as to criminalize acts which are of a certain importance. The discussions in the PrepCom have shown a general belief that no trivialization would be acceptable here. Several possibilities could be examined, one of them employed by the Egyptian-Italian proposal[3] which refers to the known formula of "sufficient gravity" in qualifying the acts constituting aggression – an idea which was taken up by the revised Greek-Portuguese[4] proposal. The Egyptian-Italian proposal even suggests criteria to decide when such gravity may be "sufficient".

This may prove useful although, on my part, I believe that it is impossible to predict all the situations which may arise, which means that we will have to deal with an illustrative list which, in its turn, means that we may have to face yet again arguments invoking contradiction with the principle of legality. Finally, it may be better to entrust the Court with the care to find what constitutes "sufficient gravity" in each particular case.

I have already mentioned the Greek-Portuguese proposal and I would like to make some brief comments on its definitional part, since the part dealing with the relationship between the ICC and the Security Council will be dealt with by other participants.

---

[2]   Encyclopaedia of Public International Law, vol. I, 1992, pp. 58-64.
[3]   A/AC.249/1997/WG.1/DP.6.
[4]   PCNICC/1999/DP.13 of 30 July 1999. See also PCNICC/2000/WGCA/DP.5 which contains the same proposal as well as an Explanatory Note prepared by the Greek legislation.

The proposal follows the "generic" approach for the reasons I have already mentioned.

Furthermore, it does not refer to the notions of "planning and preparation of war of aggression" as these phases of aggression are envisaged in article 25 of the ICC Statute which provides that criminal responsibility attaches not only to the commission of any crime under the jurisdiction of the Court, but also to those ordering, soliciting, inducing, etc. the commission of the crime, or attempting its commission.

The definition is all-inclusive, i.e., it covers all the forms of aggression which are provided for by international law today, provided that a number of conditions, which are set out in the definition, are cumulatively met. These are: a) use of armed force has taken place; b) such use of armed force is attributed to a person who holds such a position within the State undertaking the action as to exercise control or direct the political or military action of that State. Heads of State or Government, Ministers in charge of military matters, or high military authorities may be in such a position. Other officials could not be covered by this requirement; c) The use of armed force is consciously directed against the sovereignty, territorial integrity or political independence of a State; d) The use of force which has taken place violates the Charter of the United Nations. Such violation cannot, therefore, take place where the right of legitimate defense is being exercised in accordance with art. 51 of the U.N. Charter as well as where the action is taken by virtue of Chapter VII of the Charter in the exercise of collective security. This clears the situation of "humanitarian intervention", provided, of course, that it is undertaken on the basis of a Security Council resolution.

I believe that this set of conditions – with, perhaps, some minor amendments and a fair measure of fine-tuning – represents a reasonable outline of the basic concepts which must be taken up by any definition of aggression for the purposes of the Statute.

Finally, I would not like to forget that there are proposals which, by one daring stroke, incorporate the question of the relationship between the ICC and the Security Council into the definition itself. I am referring to the Russian proposal which, instead of a definition, merely uses the phrase "subject to a determination of the Security Council", together with an enumeration of forms of participation. Thus, instead of having a definition applicable to all situations, this proposal envisages an *ad hoc* approach to it, with the Security Council deciding in each particular case. Any prior attempt to a definition thus becomes redundant. It is an extreme view, which mirrors the position of certain states as regards the role of the Security Council in connection with aggression. But this is not up to me to comment.

7. Defining the Crime of Aggression or Redefining Aggression?

IOANA GABRIELA STANCU[*]

1.

First of all I would like to express my gratitude to the organizers of the conference and editors of the book for giving us the opportunity to exchange views on the crime of aggression in a more friendly environment than even the U.N. I think that this will also give our youngest participants an opportunity to see how the U.N. people start from similar departure points and arrive sometimes at completely different destinations.

2.

Reading the proposals on the crime of aggression submitted at the Preparatory Committee on the Establishment of an International Criminal Court, the United Nations Diplomatic Conference in Rome and the Preparatory Commission for the International Criminal Court (PrepCom) always offers a better understanding of the points of disagreement among delegations. Every time I'm doing this exercise I cannot help but noticing that most – if not all – of these proposals attempt to insert in the proposed *definition for the crime of aggression* a *definition of aggression*. I also notice that usually it is that very part which is the most controversial.

---

[*] Permanent Mission of Romania to the U.N., New York.

3.

Professor Shukri has said that GA resolution 3314/1974, which defines aggression, has not been successfully challenged (until we started to define the crime of aggression), if I understood him correctly. My understanding is that each of these insertions actually challenges resolution 3314. *"Defining the crime of aggression or redefining aggression"* – this seems to be the question.

Dealing with this dilemma makes it impossible to me to talk only about definition. Therefore, I apologize in advance for touching upon the conditions under which the Court shall exercise jurisdiction with respect to the crime of aggression, but definition and conditions are intrinsically linked to each other.

4.

The starting point in my analysis is the distinction between the *act of aggression*, or simply, *aggression* – as committed by the State – and the *crime of aggression* – as committed by the individual.

Aggression is prohibited by rules of international law as a conduct of a State in relation to another State. Thus, only States are capable of committing aggression, by violating these rules. A State, as we all know, is an abstract entity, behind which are individuals. Consequently, behind *aggression* committed by the State is the action of individuals who have the power to control or direct the conduct of that State, *is the crime of aggression.*

With regard to the crime of aggression, there are two aspects on which consensus among delegations participating in the PrepCom seems to be easy (or easier) to achieve:

a) that the crime of aggression is *a leadership crime*, and I am not going to insist on that, as it is widely recognized;

b) that is a *"State crime"*, meaning that we cannot speak about crime of aggression in the absence of an act of aggression; accordingly, individual, criminal responsibility for the crime of aggression presupposes that the aggression has effectively occurred, that is to say: *there could be no crime of aggression unless there is aggression.*

5.

This leads me to the idea that, as a precondition for exercising jurisdiction over the crime of aggression – which falls within the competence of the ICC – the existence of aggression should be determined – and this, I'm afraid, falls outside the competence of the ICC, as it involves the conduct of a State.

Dealing with States' responsibility is neither possible for the ICC – according to its Statute – nor desirable, not even in the case of aggression.

This is why, in my opinion, the ICC should refrain from making any determination – either directly or indirectly – of the existence of aggression.

6.

The determination of the existence of an act of aggression should be considered as a precondition for exercising the ICC's jurisdiction over the crime, that means as a procedural or preliminary condition, which should not affect the independence of the Court in determining the guilt or the innocence of the accused.

Who is in a position to make such a determination?

Romania co-sponsored a proposal together with New Zealand and Bosnia-Herzegovina during the last session of the PrepCom and intends, as it have already been announced, to revise it for the next session. What follows does not necessarily reflect an official or common position of the three delegations.

7.

According to Article 5 paragraph 2 of the Statute, the provisions establishing the conditions for the exercise of the jurisdiction of the Court over the crime of aggression "shall be consistent with the relevant provisions of the Charter of the United Nations".

There are, however, no very relevant provisions in the U.N. Charter with regard to aggression for judicial purposes.

Aggression is mentioned only in the context of establishing the rule of prohibiting it and in the context of the maintenance of international peace and security, in which the Security Council has primary responsibility.

Therefore, we have *to adapt this responsibility of the Security Council* with regard to determining aggression – *as a precondition for the actions to be taken under Chapter VII of the Charter* – to the need of determining aggression *for the purpose of ICC proceeding with criminal responsibility.*

We also have *to resort* to other bodies able to make such a determination – in case the Security Council does neither act nor react – and the International Court of Justice seems to be the best equipped for that, as the principal judicial organ of the United Nations.

8.

For this stage – determining the existence of aggression – resolution 3314 is the most important tool: it defines aggression, it is part of the customary international law, it has been designed for the Security Council, and it has been recognized and used by the International Court of Justice.

9.

Turning to the ICC, what it really needs is a definition of the crime of aggression that it could operate with, a definition focused more on the criminal behavior of the individual and less on the conduct of the State.

For the purpose of defining the crime of aggression, is it within the scope of the Statute to address the question of the definition of aggression?

Or should we focus more on the "individual who, as leader or organizer, actively participates in or orders the planning, preparation, initiation or waging of aggression committed by a State", as is the wording suggested by the International Law Commission in 1996 and drawn from the relevant provisions of the Nuremberg Charter?

In formulating these questions, I started from the assumption that:

–   the ICC is not designed to deal with aggression, only with the crime of aggression, and

–   for the purpose of individual criminal responsibility, the ICC should seek a determination of the (act of) aggression (State responsibility).

And also based on these assumptions, my preference would go to focusing on defining the crime of aggression and on that aggression that leads to criminal, individual responsibility.

10.

This should not be considered as pretending to have found the ideal solution or the magic formula. It simply is an attempt to offer another approach, a different perspective, or rather to create bridges between old and new approaches. I would be very grateful especially to those who will criticize or correct me.

8. Definition of the Crime of Aggression: State Responsibility or Individual Criminal Responsibility?

ELIZABETH WILMSHURST[*]

In the negotiations at the conference and in the different sessions of the PrepCom, a number of legal issues arising from the question of the definition of aggression are only gradually becoming apparent.

There is one legal issue that is becoming more and more prominent. The crime of aggression, more than any other of the crimes within the jurisdiction of the Court, involves the participation of a State. Of the other crimes triable by the Court, almost every one can be committed without the involvement of a State, although State participation may be more frequent than not. (If there is an exception to this it is the crime of transfer of populations into occupied territories.) But it has been generally recognized in the negotiations that the crime of aggression cannot be committed by an individual unless a State is internationally responsible for an act of aggression, however that responsibility is recognized: no State responsibility for an act of aggression, no crime of aggression by an individual. The discussion does not concern individual mercenaries who act without State backing. In seeking to find a definition we are not dealing with international responsibility but individual criminality.

This fact – which should be obvious – does give to the negotiations more of a political flavour than has been the case with the negotiation of all but a few of the other crimes within the jurisdiction of the Court. It is also capable of leading to confusion between the international law description of

---

[*] Legal Advisor, Foreign and Commonwealth Office. These remarks are made in a personal capacity and do not necessarily reflect the views of the Foreign and Commonwealth Office.

State responsibility for unlawful use of force on the one hand and the definition of the crime of aggression committed by individuals on the other. Some of the draft definitions which have been tabled in the PrepCom appear to suffer from this confusion.

It is the distinction between the two concepts (State responsibility and individual criminality) that I intend to address. The question is whether the definition of the crime of aggression committed by an individual is the same as the definition of an act of aggression committed by a State. To put the question in another way: does participation by an individual in every act of aggression or unlawful use of force committed by a State constitute a crime against peace by that individual?

To answer that question we must look to international customary law. It was international customary law that guided us in drafting definitions of the other crimes listed in the Statute; then as now we were not entirely purist in this objective, and where definitions in customary international law were not clear or certain, they had to be clarified and refined.

For the definition of the crime of aggression the starting point must be the reference to aggression in the Nuremberg Charter and Control Council Law No 10. The term in both of these texts is "war of aggression". The slightly expanded formulation in the Control Council Law does not at all change the meaning since it was quite clear that the reference was to the war or wars that had just been waged.

Moving ahead to 1974, we note that General Assembly Resolution 3314 on the definition of aggression confirms that the perception of the General Assembly in 1974 was that it was participation in a war of aggression that constituted the crime of aggression. Article 5(2) of that Resolution provides that a "war of aggression is a crime against international peace. Aggression gives rise to international responsibility." The Article thus quite clearly differentiates between aggression (which gives rise to international responsibility) and a war of aggression (which is a crime by individuals against international peace). The question has been raised as to whether the reference in that Article to a crime may have been intended as a reference to State crimes. This cannot have been the case: the concept of State crimes was extremely controversial, and the resolution would not have been adopted by consensus if there had been a reference in it to State crimes; the travaux make that clear.

The primary objective of the Resolution as a whole was to recommend the text of the Definition as a guide to the Security Council in its determination of an act of aggression by a State; this was made clear in the wording of the Resolution. That the two concepts of individual criminality and State responsibility were carefully differentiated is further borne out by statements by a number of delegates in their statements made when the Resolution was adopted, and when the definition itself was adopted in the Special Committee prior to the matter coming to the Assembly.

Apart from the Resolution there appears to be little State practice on the content of the crime of aggression. It may not be surprising that there is little, if any, evidence of domestic prosecutions by States, since aggression is considered by many to be peculiarly susceptible to *international* prosecution. As regards further international action, the draft Articles of the International Law Commission on the draft Code of Crimes against the Peace and Security of Mankind were never fully discussed by States, and neither negotiated nor adopted by them.

We are left with the result that, as far as international customary law is concerned, it is only a "war of aggression" which constitutes the crime of aggression in international law. The consequence of this is that there may be a violation by a State of an international law rule against the use of force which does not give rise to individual criminal culpability for the crime of aggression.

If the new definition of aggression is to keep to international law as it now stands, it should be confined to participation in wars of aggression, whether the term "war" is used expressly or whether an attempt is made to describe the essential elements of a war. It is undoubtedly the case that formal "wars" are rarely declared in modern times. If it should be thought that the use of the term "war" in a definition of the crime of aggression would for this reason effectively render the definition without content, we can search for a description of a "war" which captures the meaning of customary law without necessarily being confined to that word.

What is a war? What must at least be asserted is that it is not *any* unlawful use of force by a State. The mere citation of Article 2(4) of the Charter is therefore not sufficient. A border skirmish may not amount to a war. The unlawful use of force to assert unlawfully claimed fishery rights is not a war, however serious that may be for the two States concerned. Not all of the acts listed in Article 3 of the 1974 Definition of Aggression can be classed as necessarily constituting a war. However serious any of these individual acts may be, they do not comprise crimes under international law as it now stands.

In the negotiations, attempts have been made to deal with the necessity to distinguish between an act of aggression committed by a State and the crime of aggression committed by an individual. But it does not solve the problem to qualify an act as "serious" or "massive". To use such terms is neither sufficient nor necessary: not sufficient, because the seriousness of an unlawful use of force does not provide the criterion of distinction, and not necessary because the jurisdiction of the Court is already limited by Article 5 of the Statute to the most serious crimes of interest to the international community as a whole. The German draft proposal, which has now been described by its author as the "former German proposal" specified that an attack should involve a military occupation or annexation of the territory of a State. This was a good attempt to search for the essential element of an aggressive war, but for reasons explained it did not command consensus. New formulations could form the basis of a useful negotiation.

So far I have looked at the matter from the viewpoint of customary international law. But it may be asked whether from a policy point of view it would be desirable if we were to extend customary law and reject the limitation to wars of aggression. Would it be more appropriate if we were to give the Court jurisdiction over individual participation in any unlawful use of force by a State, recognizing as we must that this would involve a departure from customary law? My concern is that this approach could lead to the situation that whenever a State had a dispute with another which included use of force by that other, the State would be able to refer the situation to the international criminal court, alleging participation by individuals.

If the provisions on aggression as finally agreed would allow a State to refer any allegation of unlawful use of force by another State to the international criminal court, the court would be burdened by highly political questions which also involved complicated determinations of State responsibility. This could create in effect an inter-State court out of a court that we have all agreed should have jurisdiction only over individuals. This is not a result to be welcomed by those who have for long fought for the establishment of the court.

I conclude by answering the question I posed at the outset: does participation in *any* unlawful use of force by a State constitute the crime of aggression by an individual? I believe the answer must be no, both from a legal and policy viewpoint. The way forward is to look to customary international law and to seek a description of individual criminality based on that.

9. The Crime of Aggression: Definitional Options for the Way Forward

HANS-PETER KAUL*

I wish to start my presentation on "The Crime of Aggression – Definitional Options for the Way Forward" by simply saying: nobody should underrate the thirst of the international community for more international justice. This is also relevant with regard to the crime of aggression, in particular with regard to a definitional solution for this crime which is so grave and has, in the past, haunted so many people. Judge Jackson, the great American lawyer of the International Military Tribunal of Nuremberg, was among the first to fully understand and to appreciate this.

In my brief contribution I will present – or better recall! – in two sections, with the help of the annex to this contribution:

1. The three or four main definitional *models* for the crime of aggression;
2. Some main definitional *elements* and issues with regard to an appropriate definition.

With regard to the latter, the emphasis is on *some*, not all. And among those main definitional elements, there are some which seem more or less uncontroversial or accepted, there are others which continue to be controversial, unclear and unresolved.

In addition and very quickly, let me add three other clarifying remarks:

First, after the thorough discussions and contributions of this conference, I cannot exclude the possibility that my own contribution may be a little bit repetitive. But for the sake of analytical clarity I will simply

* Hans-Peter Kaul is Commissioner for the International Criminal Court in the German Federal Foreign Office and Head of the German ICC Delegation. The views reflected in this contribution are the author's personal ones and do not necessarily reflect those of the German Government.
The form of an oral presentation as held is maintained throughout the text.

review the main definitional models and approaches that were and continue to be discussed in the Preparatory Commission. In so far, I hope, nevertheless, that things are different if they are presented from a different angle.

Second, this also means that this time I will try to set aside my well-known role as a German delegate, who in the past five years has continuously argued for a specific approach for a definition of the crime of aggression.[1] As many of you are aware this specific approach is reflected more recently in U.N. Doc DP 4 of 13 November 2000[2] – "A further informal discussion paper" regarding the crime of aggression. If I lay out my own personal and subjective view with regard to a specific issue, I will indicate this explicitly.

Third and last introductory remark: as you are aware, as by now you all should be aware, the crime of aggression is in itself a very complex crime, namely a composite crime, a two level crime, two tier crime. In this crime – there seems now to be general agreement on this point – two main components, two essential elements must come together in order to be able to establish individual criminal responsibility:

1   There must be an illegal use of armed force, an illegal armed attack by one State against another which gives rise, according to international law, to State responsibility (and in this connection I would like to refer to Article 5 par. 2 of the Annex to GA Resolution 3314).[3]

2   There must be an individual who is in a position of control and leadership in the attacking State whose action or conduct was, at least in part, a cause for the attack in question to take place.

---

[1]   For a recent and thorough summary of the state of discussion in the Preparatory Commission see Gerd Westdickenberg, Oliver Fixson "Das Verbrechen der Aggression im Römischen Statut des Internationalen Strafgerichtshofes" in: Festschrift für Tono Eitel, forthcoming 2003, Heidelberg.

[2]   See U.N. Doc. PCNICC/2000/WGCA/DP.4.

[3]   See U.N. Doc. PCNICC/2000/WGCA.INF/1 of 27 June 2000, Reference document on the crime of aggression, prepared by the Secretariat.

At this juncture, I should like to insert a quick remark.

Let me recall the very interesting idea of our colleague Gérard Dive from Belgium put forward at the February/March PrepCom 2001 that maybe one should reflect this two level composition of the crime of aggression in an appropriate manner in a new draft structure. This would mean in concrete terms, that there would have to be an appropriate paragraph on action giving rise to State responsibility and an appropriate, but separate paragraph on the action of the individual which was causal for the armed attack. Such an approach should be further reflected upon.

***

I now turn to part one of my presentation: What are the four main definitional models which form the material for our future efforts?

Three of them you find in the two-page illustrative paper with the title "The Definition of the Crime of Aggression: Definitional Options for the Way Forward".

The fourth model, however, is still a virtual one. It is the almost magical formula of a generally acceptable definition of the crime of aggression which we have so far been unable to find. At the same time, there is hope that with assistance and gradual progress – to be promoted hopefully also through this conference – we may be able to get closer to such a generally acceptable definition.

Now, when we look at the paper, we have at first Model 1. Obviously Model 1 is based on the text of the International Military Tribunal of Nuremberg which you find in variant 1 of Model 1.[4]

Variant 2 is the Russian proposal of 1999.[5] This proposal is also based on the text of the International Military Tribunal of Nuremberg and defines the crime of aggression as planning, preparing, initiating or carrying out a war of aggression.

When we study Model 2 and the two variants contained under this heading, you are certainly aware that both variants are based on the famous text of General Assembly Resolution 3314:

– Variant A is the 1997 proposal made by Egypt and Italy which consists of a rather general, if not vague, definition of the crime of aggression

---

[4]   See *supra*, fn. 2, p. 1.
[5]   See U.N. Doc. PCNICC/1999/INF/2 of 2 August 1999, Compilation of proposals on the Crime of Aggression, p. 24.

and adds a non-exhaustive list of acts constituting aggression, taken
from Resolution 3314.[6]

– Variant B is the 1999 proposal submitted by Arab states[7], in which
Professor Shukri played an important role. This proposal is also based
on GA Resolution 3314 and it demands in particular that the use of
armed force by political or military leaders "aimed at depriving other
peoples of their rights to self-determination, freedom and
independence" shall also constitute the crime of aggression. Paragraph
2 of this proposal (variant B) is basically identical with the previous
Egyptian/Italian proposal (variant A of Model 2).

As we now turn to definitional Model 3, you could call it the
"generic approach". Here, variant A is a proposal elaborated by the German
delegation[8] – the last proposal which was under active consideration on the
table at the Rome Conference.

Now, why did I call it the former German proposal? Well, for a
variety of reasons which I would quickly like to recall. As many of you
know, the proposal contained in variant A was eventually not able to
generate general agreement in Rome and it did not achieve general
agreement later in the Preparatory Commission. Furthermore, numerous
States who at a certain time supported it as a possible compromise for the
Rome Conference later distanced themselves from it. Why? One main
reason for this distancing was the inclusion of the extraneous definitional
element "and subject to a determination by the Security Council". This
subjugation of a possible definition to a determination by the Security
Council made this variant apparently unpalatable to a number of States.
Finally, because it was emphasized many times – and also the German side
is forced to acknowledge this argument – limiting the armed attack in
question to invasion, annexation or military occupation is a somewhat
restrictive approach, probably too restrictive. It has been stressed that such
an approach does not take into account that modern mass destruction
weapons, modern weapon technology and long distance weapons make it
possible, for example, to totally destroy another country without a soldier
of the attacking State ever setting foot in the territory of the attacked State.

The last proposal under Model 3 is the Greek–Portuguese proposal[9]
(variant B). This proposal also follows the generic approach, with a rather
open definition.

---

[6] See *supra* fn. 4, pp. 3, 4.
[7] See *supra* fn. 4, p. 12.
[8] See *supra* fn. 4, pp. 10, 11.
[9] See U.N. Doc. PCNICC/2000/WGCA/DP.5, revised proposal.

***

Let me now turn to part two of my contribution, namely to a closer look at some main definitional elements. As I said before, here you can identify some definitional elements which can be regarded as more or less uncontroversial or more or less accepted. In this category I should like to highlight two definitional elements:

One, there seems to be agreement that aggression is, by definition, a leadership crime. This is currently reflected by the formula "a person who is in a position to exercise control or capable of directing political/military action in his State against another State". Here one gets the impression that this formula seems to be by and large uncontroversial. Indeed, all variants of definitional Model 2 (based on GA Resolution 3314) and definitional Model 3 (so-called "generic approach") reflect this, as they contain such a formula.

Second, there seems to be general agreement that the use of armed force or the armed attack in question must be in manifest contravention or violation of the Charter of the United Nations. While this seems to be implicit in the approach of Model 1 as described earlier, it seems to be a common feature in the definitional attempts of Model 2 and 3. Here I may add a personal view: I myself now have a certain preference for the definitional element which is contained in the Greek–Portuguese proposal[10] (Model 3, variant B) which uses the formulation "in manifest violation of the Charter of the United Nations".

***

In the final part of my contribution I will try to lead you through the deeper, difficult and more agitated waters of the issues concerning a proper definition for the crime of aggression. Here we are looking at some definitional elements and issues that are at best currently unclear, or controversial or unresolved. Here, I will concentrate on or better limit myself to four main definitional elements:

The first one is an element defining the object of the armed attack. What is the object? Is it the territorial integrity? Or is it the territorial integrity and political independence? Or is it the territorial integrity, political independence and sovereignty of the state? This is the question which must be decided. As you are aware, in the Charter of the United Nations these terms are referred to in Article 2 para. 4 dealing with the

---

[10] See *supra* fn. 8.

general prohibition to use armed force in international relations. In this respect I should like to make a remark based on common sense: it is clear that there can be no crime of aggression without violation of the territorial integrity of the attacked State. Consequently, territorial integrity must be, through obvious necessity, an indispensable object of the armed attack in question.

Second, a more difficult, more complex definitional element concerns the question of how to define the act or the conduct of the leader/perpetrator in question. In general, when we analyze the models and variants in front of us, we note that the definition taken from the Statute of the International Military Tribunal of Nuremberg, as well as the Russian proposal which is also supported by France, and the former German text, all draw on the precedent of Nuremberg. They characterize the conduct in question with the notions "to initiate, carry out, plan, prepare or order an armed attack". On the other hand, we see that the other models and variants more or less renounce a definition or a concretisation of the individual act or contribution of the leader in question.

Third, a further controversial definitional element is how to define the action of the State (not of the individual).

Should it be:

- the notion of "war" or "war of aggression"
- the notion "use of armed force" as referred to in Article 2 para. 4 of the Charter, or
- the notion of "armed attack" as referred to in Article 51 of the Charter?

The fourth, very controversial, very unresolved definitional issue in my view has to do with the quality/quantity/dimension and magnitude/intensity/gravity of the use of armed force/armed attack and the injurious consequences.

A new formula, which is now more and more familiar and frequently used by delegates in the Preparatory Commission phrases this as the so-called "threshold issue".

Now when you examine the definitional models and approaches contained in the paper in front of you, you can quite easily see that there are rather distant positions or wide disagreements in this respect:

- In Model 1 the approach is to use the notion of "war" or "war of aggression".
- In Model 2 you find the notion of the "use of armed force" combined with a list of acts as contained in GA Resolution 3314.

– The German proposal (i.e. Model 1, variant A) takes as a point of departure the notion of "armed attack" as referred to in Art. 51 of the Charter. It then stipulates that the armed attack in question must result in an "occupation or annexation". It is obvious that these two latter notions stem from GA Resolution 3314 paragraph 2 a as can be seen in definitional Model 2.

With regard to these disagreements, these unresolved issues, I should like to make a number of comments, all on a personal basis. I believe that the following should be borne in mind:

First, a norm of international criminal law establishing individual criminal responsibility must fully reflect the seriousness of the crime. Furthermore, it must – in accordance with the principle of legality – also be as clear, precise, and well-defined as possible. This requirement applies both to the illegal conduct of the State involved in a crime of aggression and to the conduct of the individual leader who is responsible for the aggression.

Second, in particular with regard to the illegal conduct of the State in question we should make a very conscious and serious effort to solve the so-called "threshold issue". In my view, we cannot do without a definitional element as clear, precise and well-defined as possible which deals with the quality, quantity, dimension, intensity, grave consequences or overall gravity of the armed attack in question.

Third, in order to emphasize this necessity and to argue for an appropriate solution Germany submitted on 13 November 2000 a further informal discussion paper on a definition for the crime of aggression as referred to in Article 5 of the Rome Statute. This document, also known as DP.4 has been mentioned by several speakers, among them Mauro Politi.

In the framework of this presentation I will not go into it again or elaborate the arguments as contained in this discussion paper. Everybody who is interested can read it. Let me simply say: the fundamental premise – I repeat: premise; this is *not* a definition – is that an aggressive, large-scale armed attack committed by a State on the territorial integrity of another State, clearly without justification under international law, represents indeed the very essence of this crime, with regard to the conduct of the aggressive State in question. In order to avoid misunderstandings let me repeat once again that this is as such not a definition for individual criminal responsibility, and we are aware of it.

***

To sum up: where does this leave us? No perfect solution is yet in sight. But again, we need as much precision and clarity as possible. Openness and vagueness are nothing for a norm of international criminal law defining the crime of aggression, which is of such enormous concern to the international community as a whole. Openness and vagueness also damage the prospects of general agreement on an appropriate definition for this crime.

To conclude, maybe I can point in the direction of two possible avenues for progress for the definitional problem.

First, how about an approach to define more precisely the magnitude and dimension and the gravity of the injurious consequences of the armed attack in question which, in our view, must be large-scale and massive.

Second, how about a formula, for example, which could read: "... An armed attack of sufficient gravity, to be comparable in magnitude, intensity and actual injurious consequences to a war, whether declared or not". Maybe we can discuss such a formula at the next PrepCom. Maybe we can even improve it.

Probably I have exhausted not only my time, but also the patience of this audience. But as a last word, let my reiterate my belief that the pending issues concerning the crime of aggression can be solved, must be solved and eventually, with patience and tenacity, will be solved.

Annex

Definitional Model 1

Variant A (International Military Tribunal Nuremberg)

The following acts, or any of them, are crimes coming within the jurisdiction of the Tribunal for which there shall be individual responsibility:

a) *Crimes against peace:* namely, planning, preparation, initiation or waging of a war of aggression, or a war in violation of international treaties, agreements or assurances, or participation in a common plan or conspiracy for the accomplishment of any of the foregoing;
...

Variant B (Russian Proposal of 29 July 1999)

For the purposes of the present Statute and subject to a prior determination by the United Nations Security Council of an act of aggression by the State concerned, the crime of aggression means any of the following acts: planning, preparing, initiating, carrying out a war of aggression.

Definitional Model 2

Variant A (Italian – Egyptian Proposal of 21 February 1997)

1. For the purposes of this Statute, the crime of aggression is committed by a person who is in a position to exercise control or capable of directing political/military actions in his State against another State, in contravention of the Charter of the United Nations, by resorting to armed force, to threaten or violate that State's sovereignty, territorial integrity or political independence.

2. Provided that the acts concerned or their consequences are of sufficient gravity, acts constituting aggression (include) (are) the following:

a) The invasion or attack by the armed forces of a State of a territory of another State, or any military occupation, however temporary, resulting from such invasion or attack, or any annexation by the use of force of the territory of another State or part thereof;

b) Bombardment by the armed forces of a State against the territory of another State, or the use of any weapons by a State against the territory of another State;

c) The blockade of the ports or coasts of a State by the armed forces of another State;

d) An attack by the armed forces of a State on the land, sea or air forces, or marine and air fleets of another State;

e) The use of armed forces of one State which are within the territory of another State with the agreement of the receiving State in contravention of the conditions provided for in the agreement, or any extension of their presence in such territory beyond the termination of the agreement;

f) The action of a State in allowing its territory, which it has placed at the disposal of another State, to be used by that other State for perpetrating an act of aggression against a third State;

g) The sending by or on behalf of a State of armed bands, groups, irregulars or mercenaries, which carry out acts of armed force against another State of such gravity as to amount to the acts listed above, or its substantial involvement therein.

Variant B (Arab Proposal of 26 February 1999)

1. For the purposes of this Statute, the crime of aggression is committed by a person who is in a position of exercising control or capable of directing political/military actions in his State, against another State, or depriving other peoples of their rights to self-

determination, freedom and independence, in contravention of the Charter of the United Nations, by resorting to armed force to threaten or to violate the sovereignty, territorial integrity or political independence of that State or the inalienable rights of those people.

2. Acts constituting aggression include the following, whether preceded by a declaration of war or not:

(a to g as in Variant A)

Definitional Model 3

Variant A (Former German Proposal of 30 July 1999)

1. For the purpose of the present Statute and subject to a determination by the Security Council referred to in article 10, paragraph 2, regarding the act of a State, the crime of aggression means either of the following acts committed by an individual who is in position of exercising control or capable of directing the political or military action of a State:
   a) initiating, or
   b) carrying out
      an armed attack directed by a State against the territorial integrity or political independence of another State when this armed attack was undertaken in manifest contravention of the Charter of the United Nations with the object or result of establishing a military occupation of, or annexing, the territory of such other State or part thereof by armed forces of the attacking State.

2. Where an attack under paragraph 1 has been committed, the
   a) planning,
   b) preparing, or
   c) ordering
      thereof by an individual who is in a position of exercising control or capable of directing the political or military action of a State shall also constitute a crime of aggression.

Variant B (Revised Greek/Portuguese Proposal of 28 November 2000)

For the purposes of the present Statute, the crime of aggression means the use of armed force (including the initiation thereof) by an individual who is in a position of exercising control or directing the political or military action of a state against the sovereignty, territorial integrity or political independence of another state (or states), in manifest violation of the Charter of the United Nations.

10. The Exercise of the International Criminal Court's Jurisdiction over the Crime of Aggression: Short Term and Long Term Prospects

ANTONIO YÁÑEZ-BARNUEVO[*]

1.

I am invited to comment on the question: "What prospects for the exercise of the International Criminal Court's jurisdiction over the crime of aggression?" Now, there are at least two possible ways of approaching the subject matter of this discussion, depending on how we interpret what is meant by that question.

One way of approaching this matter would be to indulge in an exercise of crystal-gazing, or of legal-political fiction, by trying to ascertain how the ICC might in fact operate regarding the crime of aggression, on the assumption that it would have been endowed with the jurisdiction to deal with that crime, pursuant to article 5.2 of the Rome Statute. This would certainly be a very tall order, involving superhuman abilities to look into the future, more than ten years from now – which is the minimum period for a provision on the crime of aggression to be negotiated and adopted by States and then to enter into force, according to the requirements of the Statute.

Even if one were to try to look so far ahead, there are simply too many variables involved to dare making any meaningful forecasts, as someone has not failed to point out earlier in this debate. Among those

[*] Ambassador, Head of the Spanish Delegation to the PrepCom for the ICC.

factors, I would just mention, as being particularly relevant and significant:

- what would by then be the shape of the international system of maintenance and restoration of international peace and security;
- how the provision on the crime of aggression would have been concluded: that is to say, what would be the content and reach of the definition of the crime, and which would be the conditions and modalities for the exercise of jurisdiction by the Court over it;
- how many States (and particularly, how many important countries) would have ratified, or acceded to, that provision;
- how the ICC would have succeeded by then to establish itself, assert its authority and broaden its support in the international community, especially among the most powerful countries.

2.

As those variables are too complex to analyze now in a manner that would do justice to them, I think it is preferable to interpret the question put to us in a different way: that is to say, by trying to visualize how the provision on the crime of aggression might look at the end of the negotiation and what is to be done in order to get there. For that purpose, we should concentrate, more modestly, on the road ahead of us in the immediate future, without losing sight of the horizon that we want to reach – and without forgetting either the very special characteristics of aggression among international crimes. It also goes without saying that in that endeavor our two lodestars must always be the Rome Statute and the U.N. Charter.

If we attempt to take stock of the state of things on this matter in the work already undertaken by the Preparatory Commission (PrepCom), one could say – as has been ably summarized at the beginning of this conference by Mauro Politi[1] – that the Commission has already managed to cover a lot of ground in identifying relevant issues and options, without in any way ignoring or minimizing the difficulties still outstanding.

This could certainly be asserted regarding the elements to be considered for inclusion in a definition of the crime of aggression, where a number of proposals are on the table and the main building blocks for a

---

[1]   See Politi, *The Debate within the Preparatory Commission for the International Criminal Court, supra.*

definition are well known to delegations, even if important discrepancies still remain to be overcome.[2]

In fact, we have had several rounds of a thorough discussion of those issues, especially as they concern the definition of aggression as an act of State, which is what makes aggression virtually unique among international crimes. The discussion thus far has basically centered on the elements that would make an armed attack by a State against another State an act of aggression, taking into account aspects such as its unlawfulness and its intensity or its effects.

At the last session of the PrepCom there was unanimity – reflected in the final comments by the coordinator, Silvia Fernández de Gurmendi – in considering aggression as a "leadership crime" involving only those persons who, because of their position as political or military leaders of a State, can and do take decisions directly relevant to the commission of an act of aggression by the State.

It is clear that, if no similar adjustment is expressly foreseen as regards aggression, all provisions of Part III would automatically apply to the crime of aggression whenever the relevant provision on this crime would have entered into force pursuant to article 5.2 of the Statute. Consequently, it will be necessary further to explore the implications of the consideration of aggression as a "leadership crime" from the point of view of the application of general principles of criminal law under Part III of the Statute.

In this respect, it will be extremely useful for delegations to have at their disposal a study of the case-law of international tribunals – mainly of the Nuremberg and Tokyo trials – regarding the identification in practice of the elements of individual criminal responsibility for the crime of aggression. The Spanish delegation, among others, has asked that such a study be prepared by the Secretariat, if need be with the assistance of an expert consultant, and we hope soon to receive the results of that research.

---

[2] The "Compilation of proposals on the crime of aggression" (which now should be considered as incomplete, because of the introduction of subsequent contributions by several delegations) was prepared by the Secretariat and appeared as Doc. PCNICC/1999/INF.2 of 2 August 1999. The options resulting from various proposals are contained in the "Consolidated text of proposals on the crime of aggression", prepared on the basis of the discussion paper submitted by the previous Coordinator, Mr Tuvaku Manongi, at the 3rd session of the PrepCom (Doc. PCNICC/1999/WGCA/RT.1, OF 9 December 1999). This document is reproduced in Annex V to the Proceedings of the PrepCom at its 7th session, 26 February – 9 March 2001 (Doc. PCNICC/2001/L.1/Rev.1, pp. 17-21).

3.

When we turn to the conditions for the exercise of jurisdiction by the ICC over the crime of aggression, we have to note that up to now the PrepCom has focused almost exclusively on the question of the "pre-requisite for proceeding", that is the role to be played by the Security Council or other UN organs in establishing the existence of an act of aggression by a State before the Court can address the determination of individual criminal responsibility by one or more persons. But it is my feeling that we have not sufficiently discussed other related matters, among them the application or otherwise of the principle of complementarity in this field, together with questions of admissibility of a case, as well as other jurisdictional and procedural issues.[3]

Again we have to stress that, if nothing is expressly provided for regarding the crime of aggression on these matters, all the provisions of Part II of the Rome Statute – and the rest of the Statute – would be automatically applicable also in this area. This effect, if it happens, should not just be the result of some oversight on the part of delegations, but of a deliberate decision if the negotiators come to that conclusion after serious consideration.[4]

Let me remind you in this regard that the International Law Commission, in its final draft (1996) of the Code of crimes against the peace and security of mankind, was of the opinion that the crime of aggression merited a different regime from other international crimes. Whereas for the other crimes contemplated in the draft Code the ILC suggested in draft article 8 the concurrent jurisdiction of an international criminal court and of national tribunals acting on the basis of universal jurisdiction, in the second sentence of the same provision it proposed that a future ICC be granted exclusive jurisdiction over the crime of aggression. According to the commentary of the ILC, the only exception to that general rule should be the jurisdiction of the State of nationality of the perpetrator, and that of course would only be feasible after the overthrow of the aggressor authorities through the legitimate reaction of the State victim of

---

[3]   See Escarameia, *The ICC and the Security Council: Overlapping Competencies?*, *infra*.

[4]   This list first appeared under the title "Preliminary list of possible issues relating to the crime of aggression" as a discussion paper proposed by the coordinator, Mr. Manongi, at the 4th session of the PrepCom (Doc. PCNICC/2000/WGCA/RT.1, of 29 March 2000). It is also reproduced in Annex V to the Proceedings of the PrepCom at its 7th session (doc. PCNICC/2001/L.1/Rev.1, pp. 22-24). In order better to understand he meaning and intent of that list, it is interesting to read it together with the Suggestions made orally by Italy on 13 March 2000 with regard to a structure for discussion on the crime of aggression" (Doc. PCNICC/2000/WGCA/DP.3, of 24 March 2000).

the aggression, through collective action of the international community or through internal upheaval in the State concerned.[5]

Going even further, I believe that we should also ask ourselves about other possible consequences for the functioning of the ICC system when addressing the crime of aggression, precisely because of its unique characteristics among international crimes. We should reflect, for instance, on the role to be accorded to interested States in the course of the proceedings, on the effects of the relevant provision on the rights of the accused when raising defenses, even on the possibility of having enlarged chambers to deal with this kind of crime.

When I refer to these aspects, it is partly because I'm convinced that the special nature of the crime of aggression will require particular provisions or arrangements in a number of areas. But it is also because I feel that a general agreement could perhaps be fostered if we explore other avenues which could assist in accommodating the apprehensions of a number of delegations that are not yet convinced of the desirability or feasibility of including the crime of aggression within the effective jurisdiction of the ICC.

4.

Let me turn now to the prospects for the short and medium-term future of the work of the PrepCom in this field, and here I dare to speak, of course, under the control of the able and expert Coordinator for this item, Silvia Fernández de Gurmendi. I will try to distinguish the more substantive aspects of the negotiation from a purely procedural one, which affects the whole of the process.

Addressing the points of substance in the first place, it is my feeling that in the next stages of the negotiation the PrepCom should try to do the following things:

a) Complete the examination of the aspects regarding individual criminal responsibility for the crime of aggression, basing ourselves on the study to be submitted to the Secretariat on the relevant case-law by

---

[5]   Cf. the relevant section of the report of the International Law Commission to the U.N. General Assembly on the work of its 48th session, 6 May – 26 July 1996 (doc. A/51/10), PP. 42 – 55.

international tribunals. In relation with this, it would probably be fruitful to explore further the Belgian idea to distinguish, within the definition, between the individual aspect and the act-of-State aspect of the crime.

b) Attempt to reduce the number of options still existing as to the definition of the act of aggression by a State, and in so doing to delve into the possibility of introducing a gravity threshold, as has been suggested by a number of delegations (and has been very cogently explained here by Hans-Peter Kaul).

c) Continue to explore possible and workable alternatives to the exclusive determination by the Security Council of an act of aggression by a state in so far as it concerns the exercise of jurisdiction over that crime by the ICC.

On the basis of this work, it would be necessary, at some point in the medium term, to try to put together all these elements, as well as some others – as I have tried to show earlier – into a sort of "consolidated negotiating text" covering the whole of the provision on the crime of aggression to be submitted eventually to a review conference. This text, which at the beginning would inevitably contain alternatives and variants inserted between brackets, would help in concentrating the minds of negotiators and offer a clearer view of a possible outcome.

It should never be forgotten that, from the way article 5.2 of the Statute is drafted, any provision in the crime of aggression will have to be adopted and accepted by States *in toto*. Moreover, it could well be that there are potential trade-offs involved in considering together, at the appropriate time, both the definition of the crime and the conditions for the exercise of jurisdiction by the Court. Therefore, the only way to have a viable provision on the crime of aggression at the end of the process will be by crafting a "package deal" that proves to be generally acceptable to delegations.

5.

Now about the procedural point I was referring to, which could affect the whole of the negotiating process.[6] For the moment, according to Resolution F of the Rome Conference, we are working on this very important matter in

---

[6]   This point was raised in a non-paper prepared by the working group of NGOs on the crime of aggression, which was informally distributed to delegations at the 7th session of the PrepCom (March 2001).

the framework of the PrepCom, which is open practically to all States, even if they have not ratified, or even signed, the Rome Statute. It is encouraging to note that many of those non-contracting States are in fact taking an active part in the deliberations of the PrepCom on this item, and I am alluding both to permanent members of the Security Council and to countries belonging to the Non-Aligned Movement.

Of course, according to article 5.2 of the Statute and Resolution F, if and when a complete draft proposal on the crime of aggression is finally prepared it would have to be submitted to a review conference, with a view to arriving at an acceptable provision on that crime for its inclusion in the Statute following the procedures set out in articles 121 and 123 for the amendments to it. But what would happen if the PrepCom were not able to agree during its lifetime on a common proposal for such a provision? This is not an implausible hypothesis, to say the least, and we should begin reflecting upon it.

Let us recall that the PrepCom, under Resolution F, is only to function until the first session of the Assembly of States Parties to the Statute. Once it will have prepared the various draft instruments and other arrangements it was asked to do and after it will have submitted its report to the Assembly, the PrepCom will come to an end. This could happen as soon as next year, when the required 60 ratifications or accessions are expected to be met; after that, the Statute will enter into force and the Assembly of States Parties will be convened by the U.N. Secretary General.

In such a situation, absent an agreed proposal on the crime of aggression, we would face two different, inter-related problems. On the one hand, Resolution F only refers to the role to be played by the PrepCom in this regard, although it also adds that the PrepCom would have "to submit such proposals to the Assembly of States Parties at a review conference..." (which is already a rather ambiguous, or even incorrect, urn of phrase). On the other hand, while the PrepCom is open to the equal participation of practically all States, the Assembly, under article 112 of the Statute, will have only States Parties as full members, with other States – signatories of the Statute or the Final Act of the Rome Conference – entitled to attend as observers, with the right to speak but not to vote.

Of course, the PrepCom should try to advance as much as possible on this matter during its lifetime, in order to consolidate and deepen the progress that has already been made. But, if no overall agreed solution can be reached by the moment the Statute enters into force, then the PrepCom should recommend that the work on the crime of aggression be continued within the framework of the Assembly of States Parties. One could very well envisage a special working group to be established under the aegis of the Assembly, which should be open not only to States Parties but to all States, or at least to Observer States as well. In this field even more than in others relating to the development of the Statute, it is of the utmost importance to count on the full participation of all States and groups of States. For the same reason, that working group of the Assembly should work, as is the case with the present working group within the PrepCom, on the basis of consensus or the widest possible degree of agreement among delegations.

6.

In concluding, let me put forward some reflections for the long term of our endeavors concerning the crime of aggression.

In the first place, I believe that we should not expect too much from the ICC in dealing with the crime of aggression. In particular, we should not expect the Court to do what it cannot possibly do. It is clear that the Court could not by itself check aggression, defeat aggression or roll back the effects of aggression. In the future, let us hope the Court could deal with the determination of individual criminal responsibilities deriving from acts of aggression; but it could only perform that function in an effective manner once those acts of aggression have been defeated and overturned with the assistance of the international community or, as the case may be, through an internal upheaval provoking a change of regime in the aggressor State.

This brings out the inevitable conclusion that, in order to be effective in dealing with the crime of aggression, the ICC will require – even more than for the other crimes within its jurisdiction – the full support of the international community, and particularly of the Security Council, even if the Council does not have a monopoly on the determination of an act of aggression. The alternative would be for the ICC to become a sort of purely moral instance such as the so-called Russell Tribunal a few decades ago, which is certainly not what we are looking for.

An adequate response to aggression will also be required on the part of everybody concerned – the ICC, the Security Council, the General Assembly. The international community as a whole – a greater willingness to call a spade a spade, even more than has been the case thus far. That is to say, international bodies have to gather the moral courage in specific cases to call aggression, or to call genocide or crime against humanity atrocities that are clearly such – and then be prepared collectively to do whatever is necessary to deal effectively with those heinous crimes and their terrible consequences.

In particular, we have to recognize that the record of the Security Council in this respect leaves much to be desired. Not even in the glaring cases of the invasion of South Korea by North Korea in 1950, or of Kuwait by Iraq in 1990, did the Council formally determine the existence of an act of aggression, even if it treated the respective attacks practically to the same effect. And this reluctance to pronounce itself in a clear and forceful fashion when the world was expecting its supreme guidance was disgracefully repeated by the Council for a few fateful and critical weeks when a country-wide genocide was being perpetrated in Rwanda in the spring of 1994.

The world could hardly find its way to durable justice and peace with such an abdication of responsibility on the part of those who have to exercise power and leadership. Let us always recall what the sage said: "To be able to name things is the first step to apprehend them and to master them."

THE CRIME OF AGGRESSION AND THE RELATIONSHIP BETWEEN THE INTERNATIONAL CRIMINAL COURT AND THE SECURITY COUNCIL

11. The Respective Roles of the ICC and the Security Council in Determining the Existence of an Aggression

GIORGIO GAJA[*]

1.

The compromise solution that was reached at the Rome Conference with regard to aggression includes the specification in Article 5(2) that the amendment "defining the crime and setting out the conditions under which the Court shall exercise jurisdiction with respect to this crime" should be "consistent with the relevant provisions of the Charter of the United Nations". This clearly concerns the respective findings by the Security Council and the Court that a State or another entity has or has not committed aggression. For the Court a finding to this end is essential because a crime of aggression would be inconceivable under international law without a State or another entity having committed aggression.

Coordinating the roles of the two bodies was the question that the International Law Commission had attempted to resolve in its draft Statute by making a determination by the Security Council a condition for the Court to be able to try an individual for aggression.[1] Similarly, some delegations in the Preparatory Committee held that the "Security Council

---

[*]   Professor of International Law, University of Florence. Member of the International Law Commission. This is an amended and updated version of part of a chapter of the commentary on the ICC Statute edited by A. Cassese, P. Gaeta and J. Jones (Oxford University Press, 2002). The text corresponds in substance to part of the oral presentation made at the Trento conference.
[1]   *Yearbook of the International Law Commission*, 1994, II, 2.

has the exclusive power to determine whether an act of aggression has been committed".[2]

At the Rome Conference Cameroon proposed to say in Article 10(1) of the Statute that "[t]he Security Council shall determine the existence of aggression in accordance with the pertinent provisions of the Charter of the United Nations before any proceedings take place in the Court in regard to a crime of aggression".[3] Two proposals made to the Preparatory Commission after the Conference follow the same line. The Russian Federation proposed a definition of aggression that was made "subject to a prior determination by the United Nations Security Council".[4] A similar proposal was made by Germany.[5]

According to two more recent proposals the Security Council is not given an exclusive role. A text submitted by Greece and Portugal envisages that "[t]he Court shall exercise its jurisdiction with regard to this crime subject to a determination by the Security Council, in accordance with Article 39 of the Charter, that an act of aggression has been committed by the State concerned"; should the Council not yet have made such a determination, the Court will make a request to this end. However, according to the same proposal, "[i]f the Security Council does not make such a determination or does not make use of Article 16 of the Statute within 12 months of the request, the Court shall proceed with the case in question".[6] A later proposal, submitted by Bosnia and Herzegovina, New Zealand and Romania, offers a variation of the same approach, by stating that "[w]here the Security Council makes no such determination, or does not invoke Article 16, within twelve months from the date of notification by the Court, the Court may notify the General Assembly of the situation before the Court and invite the General Assembly to request the International Court of Justice, in accordance with Article 96 of the Charter, to give an advisory opinion on the legal question of the existence or otherwise of an act of aggression by the State concerned"; only if the ICJ "delivers an advisory opinion that there has been an act of aggression by

---

[2]   *Report of the Preparatory Committee on the Establishment of an International Criminal Court,* Doc. A/51/22, p. 32.

[3]   Doc. A/CONF.183/C.1/L.39. The proposal included a paragraph which stated that, if the Security Council delayed a reply to the Court's request for a declaration on the existence of aggression, the Court could "commence an investigation for the purpose of establishing whether a crime of aggression within the meaning of the present Statute exists".

[4]   Doc. PCNICC/1999/DP.12.

[5]   Doc. PCNICC/1999/DP.13.

[6]   Doc. PCNICC/2000/WGCA/DP.5.

the State concerned, and the General Assembly so recommends" may the ICC proceed.[7]

2.

When one considers the role of the various U.N. organs with regard to the determination of aggression, it may be said that the U.N. Charter "specifically assigned that function to the Council".[8] This is because aggression is one of the pre-conditions for the Security Council to be entitled to use its powers under Chapter VII of the U.N. Charter. However, it could not be argued that under the Charter the Security Council has been given an exclusive power to take a decision on the existence of aggression, nor that a finding by the Security Council would have to be binding also for a treaty body entrusted with the repression of individual crimes. Any such binding effect is not required under Article 103 of the U.N. Charter or under Article 5(2) of the ICC Statute, but is only one of the ways in which a link between the Security Council and the ICC could be established.

3.

Should one consider that the Court could make an independent finding on whether aggression has taken place, the Court's determination would have no legal consequence for the Security Council. Even the political pressure that such a finding could cause on the Security Council would be limited.[9] Conflicting findings on aggression – a positive determination by the Court and a negative one by the Council, or vice versa – could well occur. It would certainly be desirable to find ways to prevent a conflict from

---

[7] Doc. PCNICC/2001/WGCA/DP.1.

[8] See B. Ferencz, "Getting Aggressive About Preventing Aggression", 6 *Brown Journal of World Affairs* (1999) 87-96.

[9] A. Carpenter, "The International Criminal Court and the Crime of Aggression", 64 *Nordic Journal of International Law* (1995) 223 at 233 noted that "the Security Council's peace making efforts could be constrained if it were possible for the Court to commence prosecutions against aggressors independent of, or concurrent with, peace making activities". According to J. Hogan-Doran and B. van Ginkel, "Aggression as a Crime under International Law and the Prosecution of Individuals by the Proposed International Criminal Court", 43 *Netherlands International Law Review* (1996) 321 at 346, "whatever the short-term or conflict-specific concerns about the interference of the Court's role in the peace-making activities of the Security Council, in the longer term the consensus of opinion is that it can only serve to reduce the resort to armed conflict by States".

occurring. On the other hand, it also appears desirable not to tie the Court to a previous assessment by the Security Council. Any of the permanent members of the Council would otherwise be entitled to prevent the ICC from taking criminal proceedings on aggression. Moreover, the Security Council, in case of a positive finding, would impinge on the Court's judicial function, since an aggression necessarily implies that at least some of the leaders of the aggressor State are criminally responsible.

The most likely occurrence would be that the Council does not find that aggression has occurred. In 55 years of activity, with the sole exception of Res. 387 (1976) which condemned "South Africa's aggression against the People's Republic of Angola", the SC has never found that aggression has taken place. Even Iraq's invasion of Kuwait was only defined as a "breach of the peace" in SC Res. 661 (1990). Preambular paragraphs in SC Res. 418 (1977) and 527 (1982) referred to South Africa's "aggressive acts" on its neighboring States and on Namibia, but the Council still found that there only was a threat to the peace. The Security Council's tendency to understate its evaluation of the situation obviously finds its origin in the difficulty that the Security Council would otherwise have in reaching the required majority for adopting a resolution. It is therefore clear that making the Court's finding on aggression dependent on a previous assessment by the Security Council to the same effect would deprive the provision on aggression in the ICC Statute of almost all its meaning.

Moreover, one cannot assume that when the Security Council uses its powers under Chapter VII on a basis which is alternative to aggression, the Council necessarily takes a negative view on the existence of aggression. The Council's powers are not in any way affected; downgrading in the text of a resolution a situation of aggression to a breach of the peace or even to a threat to the peace may be due only to considerations of political expediency. Thus one cannot assume that the absence of a finding by the Security Council that aggression occurred necessarily implies that in the Security Council's view there is no aggression and that therefore a conflict would arise with a positive finding by the ICC that an individual has committed a crime of aggression.

12. Reflections on the Role of the Security Council in Determining an Act of Aggression

SAEID MIRZAEE YENGEJEH[*]

Article five of the Rome Statute ("the Statute") of the International Criminal Court ("the Criminal Court") enumerates the crimes that fall within the jurisdiction of the Criminal Court, including the crime of aggression. The Criminal Court shall exercise its jurisdiction with respect to the crime of genocide, crimes against humanity and war crimes, upon its establishment following entering into force of the Statute. By contrast, the Criminal Court will not be in a position to exercise its jurisdiction with regard to the crime of aggression once it is established. The Criminal Court shall exercise its jurisdiction over the crime of aggression, only after a definition for the crime of aggression is agreed and adopted by the first review conference[1] of the Rome Statute. Moreover, a definition of the crime of aggression should be accompanied by a formulation on the relationship of the Security Council with the Criminal Court, which should be consistent with the relevant provisions of the Charter of the United Nations.

The Preparatory Commission of the International Criminal Court has been entrusted by the Resolution F, adopted by the Rome Diplomatic Conference, to prepare the following provisions concerning the crime of aggression, which should be approved by the review conference of the States Parties to the Statute.

---

[*] Permanent Mission of the Islamic Republic of Iran to the U.N., New York.
[1] The first review conference of the Statute shall be convened seven years after the entry into force of the Statute. See Article 123 of the Statute.

- Definition of aggression
- Elements of the crime of aggression
- Condition under which the Criminal Court should exercise its jurisdiction with regard to this crime.

I shall not address the question of the definition of aggression, since I believe the General Assembly Resolution 3314, adopted in 1974, provides for a sound basis for negotiations and agreement on the definition of aggression in the context of ICC Statute. Likewise, I shall not touch upon the related issue of the elements of crime for the crime of aggression. These elements could be prepared once an agreement on the definition itself is clear. Consequently, I shall attempt to elaborate the relationship of the Security Council with the Criminal Court in respect of the determination of an act of aggression. Certainly, progress on this hard core question would, to a large extent, facilitate the task of the Preparatory Commission in fulfilling its mandate, which is an unconditional assignment and must be accomplished within the life span of the Preparatory Commission.[2]

The latter part of paragraph 2 of Article 5 of the Statute stipulates that a provision on the relationship of the Security Council with the Criminal Court "shall be consistent with the relevant provisions of the Charter of the United Nations". This condition is consistent with Article 103 of the Charter of the United Nations, which accords priority to the obligations of States arising out of the Charter in comparison to their commitments emanating from other international instruments. As a consequence, any provision on the relationship of the Security Council and the Criminal Court on the crime of aggression should be developed within the existing parameters, namely, U.N. Charter and the Statute.

As far as Charter provisions are concerned, Article 39 bears particular relevance to the subject under discussion. The Security Council has the responsibility, under Article 39, to determine the commission of an act of aggression by the State concerned. If the Council fulfills the mandate entrusted to it and determines the State that committed aggression, then the Criminal Court would be in a position to prosecute and punish individuals for the role they have played in launching an aggression. This is an ideal scenario, and if materialized, it would facilitate, to a large extent, the

---

[2]   Resolution F adopted by the Rome Diplomatic Conference stipulates in paragraph 7: "The Commission shall prepare proposals for a provision on aggression, including the definition and Elements of Crime of aggression and conditions under which the International Criminal Court shall exercise its jurisdiction with regard to this crime."

prosecution of those individuals that prepare, plan or commit an act of aggression.

However, those who have followed the negotiations on the crime of aggression, either during the Rome Diplomatic Conference or in the discussions that followed in the Preparatory Commission, will appreciate that the question of the relationship of the Criminal Court with the Security Council is not as simple as mentioned. Obviously our world is not a perfect one and therefore we cannot rely on ideal scenarios. We are living in a world where aggressions have taken place, norms and principles of international humanitarian law have been grossly violated, but perpetrators of such heinous crimes have not been brought to justice. Therefore, scenarios to be prepared for upholding justice must take into consideration the existing realities. The question of failure of the Security Council in dealing with the determination of acts of aggression should be addressed in any formulation on the relationship of the Security Council with the Criminal Court concerning the crime of aggression. The point needs to be clarified that in cases of inaction by the Council or its failure to ascertain the aggressor, what remedies anticipated in the Charter provisions and what kind of conclusions could be deduced from the United Nations practice.

Article 39 of the Charter, has empowered the Security Council to determine, including *inter alia*, the commission of an act of aggression. It is not understood from the letter and spirit of this Article that powers bestowed upon the Security Council are exclusive. It might be argued however, that the primary responsibility for the maintenance of international peace and security conferred on the Security Council in accordance with Article 24 of the Charter. Consequently, the council should play a prominent role in deciding the commission of an act of aggression. This assumption requires some comments.

First, the "primary responsibility" of the Security Council in respect of the maintenance of international peace and security is not an exclusive power. This issue has been discussed in the General Assembly in the course of the debate prior to the adoption of the famous Uniting for Peace Resolution. In the course of that debate, the United States argued that while "primary" responsibility for the maintenance of international peace and security rests with the Security Council, its responsibility was not exclusive.[3] In the view of the United States, in addition to Articles 11 and 14 of the Charter, Article 10 gave the General Assembly the right to make recommendations to Member States on any matter within the scope of the Charter. The United Kingdom delegate pointed out, during the same debate,

---

[3] See Eric Stein and Richard C. Morrissey, "Uniting for Peace Resolution", *Encyclopedia of Public International Law*, Vol. 5, p. 380.

that if there was breach of the peace, it was natural that under Article 11(2) the question should be referred to the Security Council. The British delegate further observed that if the Security Council did not exercise its powers, Article 11 would not preclude the General Assembly from using the powers conferred to it by Article 10.[4]

The question of the "primary responsibility" has also been examined by the International Court of Justice in the Case concerning Certain Expenses of the United Nations. The ICJ observed in this respect that the primary responsibility does not necessarily mean exclusive authority.[5] ICJ elaborated on the nature of the primary responsibility and maintained:

> This primary responsibility is conferred upon the Security Council, as stated in Article 24, "in order to ensure prompt and effective action." To this end, it is the Security Council, which is given a power to impose an explicit obligation of compliance if for example, it issues an order or command to an aggressor under chapter VII. It is only the Security Council, which can require enforcement by coercive action against an aggressor.[6]

Thus, in the view of ICJ the primary responsibility has been granted to the council to maintain peace and security by taking action against those that infringe the fundamental norms and principles of international law including those who resort to the use of force. Obviously, insensitivity of the Council or its failure to promptly and positively react, in cases of commission of an act of aggression, cannot be justified under the guise of the primary responsibility. Nor can the paralysis of the Council prevent the Organization from discharging its responsibility under the Charter.

Second, Charter provisions have made it abundantly clear that the General Assembly should also be concerned with the maintenance of international peace and security. Article 14 of the Charter authorizes the Assembly to make recommendations as to the measures that should be adopted for the peaceful settlement of disputes that are likely to impair friendly relations among nations. As ICJ has observed, "the word measures imply some kind of action"[7] to be taken by the General Assembly. The only limitation that Article 14 imposes on the General Assembly is found in

---

[4]   *Yearbook of the United Nations*, 1950, p.187.
[5]   Reports of Judgments and Advisory Opinions and orders of the International Court of Justice, 1962, p. 163.
[6]   *Ibid*.
[7]   *Ibid*.

Article 12 of the Charter. The Assembly should not recommend measures while the Security Council is dealing with the same matter unless the Council requests to do so.

Third, the question of paralysis of the Council caused by lack of unanimity among the permanent members of the council has been dealt with in the Uniting for Peace Resolution adopted by the General Assembly in 1950.[8] Part A of that resolution provides that if the Security Council, because of lack of unanimity of the permanent members, fails to exercise its primary responsibility for the maintenance of international peace and security the General Assembly shall consider the matter immediately. That resolution has been invoked on several occasions to convene the Emergency Special Session of the General Assembly. The Security Council itself on a number of cases has invoked Uniting for Peace Resolution and called for the Emergency Special Session of the General Assembly.[9] A number of measures have been adopted by the Special Emergency Sessions so convened and some recommendations have been made concerning the maintenance of international peace and security.[10]

As a result of the above points it could be firmly stated that, although the determination of an act of aggression is a primary responsibility given to the Council, it is not an exclusive one. At least in one case the Security Council itself has given an indication that the powers conferred on it could be relegated to an impartial body. Paragraph six of the Security Council resolution 598 requested the Secretary-General "to explore, in consultation with Iran and Iraq, the question of entrusting an impartial body with inquiring into responsibility for the conflict".[11]

---

[8]   General Assembly Resolution 377 (V) 3 November 1950.

[9]   Yugoslavia in 1956 suggested the first such session to consider the Suez Canal crisis. (S Res 119 (1956)), Uniting for Peace resolution has been invoked in 1956 in Hungarian crisis (S/Res/120), Lebanese crisis in 1958 (S/Res/129), Congo problem in 160 (S/Res/157), Bangladesh problem in 1971 (S/Res/303), intervention in Afghanistan in 1980 (GA Res. ES-6/2)

[10]   See Eric Stein and Richard C. Morrissey, "Uniting for Peace Resolution", *Encyclopedia of Public International Law*, Vol. 5, pp.379-382.

[11]   The Secretary General in compliance with that resolution and after consultations with the parties, examination of all relevant information contained in the official documents of the United Nations, and the information obtained from independent experts, reported to the Security Council that "Iraq's aggression against Iran" was unjustifiable. He declared that "Iraq's continuous occupation of Iranian territory during the conflict" was in violation of the prohibition of the use of force, which is regarded as one of the rules of *jus cogens*. See Further Report of the Secretary-General on the Implementation of the Security Council Resolution 598 (1987), U.N. Document S/23273, 9 December 1991.

The above mentioned resolution reflects the fact that after seven years of deliberations, the Security Council failed to determine the aggressor, on political grounds, who initiated the conflict and occupied parts of Iranian territory in the early stages of the war. This is another indication supporting the argument that the question of the determination of aggression has not solely been granted to the Council, and that there are exceptions to its authority.

This perception is also compatible with paragraph (a) of Article 13 of the Statute. Since, it has foreseen a situation where the Security Council itself may refer a situation to the Criminal Court, in which one or more of the crimes within the jurisdiction of the Criminal Court appears to have been committed. There is no reason to believe that, once the definition of aggression in the context of the Statute is clear, the Security Council cannot refer a situation to the Criminal Court, where the crime of aggression is believed to have been committed. Such referral would be compatible with the Charter provisions as well as the relevant provisions of the Statute.

It is also essential that a balanced relationship can envisage a situation where the Security Council fails to determine the commission of an act of aggression. If an aggression takes place and the Security Council, on political grounds, fails to recognize the aggressor State, this question should be referred to an impartial body. There are three possible ways in dealing with this thorny issue.

In accordance with one view, the General Assembly can play a role in cases of the failure of the Council in determining the aggressor. Proponents of this view believe that in cases of the failure of the Council the Uniting for Peace Resolution should be invoked to convene the Special Emergency Session of the General Assembly to make a recommendation on the commission of an act of aggression.

There is already another proposal on the table, requiring the International Court of Justice to make a ruling in such circumstances. The proposal submitted by Bosnia and Herzegovina, Romania and New Zealand seeks to request the advisory opinion of the International Court of Justice in case of failure of the Council in discharging its responsibility in respect of the commission of an act of aggression.[12]

The third possible solution could be to assign the Criminal Court itself to make a ruling in the absence of the determination by the Security Council. Two proposals submitted by the delegations of Colombia, and by Greece and Portugal provide for the ruling of the Criminal Court, in the absence of determination by the Security Council.[13]

---

[12] PCNICC/2001/WGCA/DP.1.

[13] See documents PCNICC/2000/WGCA/DP.5, and PCNICC/2000/WGCA/DP.1.

Opting for one solution out of three is a political decision that should be made by the Member States of the United Nations. As far as the substance of the proposals are concerned, each one of the above mentioned approaches has its own merits. At this stage, I can only express my own views on an individual capacity.

Referral of the question of lack of decision by the Security Council to the General Assembly, by invoking the Uniting for Peace Resolution is an option, which has a basis in the Charter and also in the practice of the United Nations. For historical reasons the composition of the Security Council does not represent the current membership of the United Nations. In such circumstance, a recommendation from the General Assembly, embodying the entire membership of the United Nations, should be acceptable to all its members. Therefore, if the Members of the United Nations so decide, a formulation on the basis of the practice of the United Nations could be developed.

Requesting an advisory opinion from the International Court of Justice concerning determination of an act of aggression is another option, which is based on Article 96 of the Charter. The International Court of Justice is the judicial organ of the United Nations. Both the Security Council and the General Assembly have the competence to request an advisory opinion, on any legal question, from the International Court of Justice. If the Council fails to make a decision on an aggression, and if it does not make a request for an advisory opinion from the ICJ, the Uniting for Peace Resolution could be invoked to request an advisory opinion. The advantages of this procedure are twofold. First, it is based on the Charter provisions. Second, ICJ is the judicial organ of the Organization and has the competence to provide an impartial and independent advisory opinion.

In accordance with the third option, the Criminal Court itself should make a ruling as to the determination of aggressor in cases of failure of the Council. It has to be emphasized that the Criminal Court would comprise of 18 judges to be elected "from among persons of high moral character, impartiality and integrity" who possess the qualification required to be appointed "to the highest judicial offices".[14] There is no reason to believe that such a court would not be in a position to render a judgment in cases of alleged commission of an act of aggression. Moreover, as I stated earlier, the Statute itself has prescribed in Article 13(a) that the Security Council itself may refer a situation to the Criminal Court, in which one or more of the crimes within the jurisdiction of the Criminal Court appears to

---

[14] Article 36, paragraph 3(a) of the Statute.

have been committed. There is no reason to believe that a situation in which the crime of aggression is believed to have been committed, could not be referred to the Criminal Court by the Security Council.

Furthermore, Article 16 of the Statute stipulates that the Security Council, acting under chapter seven of the Charter, could defer the investigation or prosecution of alleged commission of the crimes by the Criminal Court. Once the jurisdiction of the Criminal Court with regard to the crime of aggression becomes operational, the said provision would also be applicable to the proceedings of the Criminal Court concerning the crime of aggression. This formulation, which has not made any differentiation between the crime of aggression and other crimes within the jurisdiction of the Criminal Court, takes into consideration the powers entrusted to Council in respect of the maintenance of international peace and security.

Last but not the least, the Criminal Court must apply one unified regime concerning its relationship with the Security Council. It seems imprudent to formulate different provisions to be applicable to the relationship of the Criminal Court with the Security Council in respect of the crime of aggression on the one hand, and separate regime to be applied to the relationship of the same bodies concerning other crimes within the jurisdiction of the Criminal Court. Thus for practical reasons and for the sake of avoiding further perplexing this complex issue, it seems prudent to empower the Criminal Court to make a ruling in cases of failure of the Security Council in determining the aggressor, after the elapse of a specified period of time.

13. The ICC and the Security Council on Aggression: Overlapping Competencies?

PAULA ESCARAMEIA[*]

Introductory Note

I believe that to deal with the issue of aggression, as in so many areas related to the International Criminal Court (ICC), such as constitutional conformity or the practical application of the Statute, it is essential to view the Court against the background of our present world legal order. In fact, we no longer live in a world whose power is exclusively shared by territorial sovereign entities, i.e. the States, but, at the same time, we do not inhabit a world dominated by other entities, such as groups or individuals or companies, for example. Our post-Westphalian times are fundamentally a mixture of tendencies and the new model that emerges will depend on which of them prevail.[1]

One of the practical problems we often face nowadays is that of trying to get guidance from the old familiar model to solve new problems that have arisen up recently, such as, for instance, when new institutions are set up to address issues that were not at the center of international concerns in the past. The ICC might be the most paradigmatic of such institutions,

[*] Professor of International Law, University of Lisbon. Although the author has been a member of the Portuguese delegation to the negotiations on the International Criminal Court, the views in this article are expressed in her academic capacity and are, therefore, only her own.
[1] This theme has been present in international legal scholarship for some time now, one of its first proponents being Richard Falk, in works such as *Revitalizing International Law*, Iowa State University Press, Ames, Iowa, 1989. International Relations theorists and political scientists have also embraced this shift in paradigm from states or nations to other entities. Among others, Samuel Huntington, in articles such as "The Clash of Civilizations?" *Foreign Affairs*, Vol. 72 No. 3, Summer 1993.

since its main purpose is to deter and punish individuals who commit the most serious crimes, thus putting at the center of world regulation the protection of human victims and the vindication of their rights and reflecting a new, growing intolerance towards some abuses of power.

The consensus that is present nowadays concerning the need for criminal punishment of the perpetrators of such crimes is often in search of sources of legitimacy from the previous model, which might be a wise step for a smooth transition. However, problems often occur because previous legal instruments and institutions were not conceived and not built with these concerns in mind and they present a range of possible interpretations that do not give a clear answer. This situation has been very present in the harmonization of national Constitutions with the Statute[2] and is also present in the efforts to find in the U.N. Charter and other documents answers to the question of aggression. To put it simply, these instruments do not address our questions of international individual criminal responsibility and their guidance can never be clear and undisputed in this matter.

Therefore, I consider that a healthy departure point for the whole debate on the conditions for the exercise of the crime of aggression is the realization that the Charter did not take into account this issue and that the organic structure and mechanisms it set up did not have the question of the criminal punishment of individuals in mind. A following healthy step is, thus, to go back to our sources.

What we can be sure of is that the Charter deals with questions of use of force (art. 2(4)), maintenance of international peace and security (arts. 11, 12 and 24, among others) and threats and breaches of peace and aggression (art. 39) and that the Rome Statute states, in art. 5(2), that the Court shall exercise jurisdiction over the crime of aggression once the definition and conditions for exercise are adopted through an amendment of the Statute which must be consistent with the U.N. Charter. Furthermore,

---

[2] For an overview of potential problems arising from the compatibility of national constitutions with the Rome Statute, see, among others, Kress, Claus and Lattanzi, Flavia eds. *The Rome Statute and Domestic Legal Orders – vol. I*, Nomos Verlagsgessellschaft, Il Sirente, Baden-Baden, 2000; Duffy, Helen "National Constitutional Compatibility and the International Criminal Court", *Duke Journal of Comparative and International Law*, December 2000/January 2001; for an overview of the issues in countries members of the Council of Europe, see "Report on Constitutional Issues raised by the Ratification of the Rome Statute of the International Criminal Court", adopted by the European Commission for Democracy through Law, 45th Plenary Meeting, Venice, 15-16 December 2000. For a look at the situation in the Andean countries, see *La Corte Penal Internacional y los Paises Andinos*, Comisión Andina de Juristas, Peru, 2001. The constitutional provisions that have most frequently posed problems are those stating the immunities of power-holders, the prohibition of extradition of nationals and, in some Iberian and Latin American countries, the prohibition of life imprisonment.

we know that the Preparatory Commission must carry out its mandate, according to res. F of the Rome Conference, of preparing "proposals for a provision on aggression, including the definition and Elements of Crimes of aggression and the conditions under which the International Criminal Court shall exercise its jurisdiction with regard to this crime".

The ICC Statute and the UN Charter

Going back to the sources and at the cost of repetition, let us look at what the Charter tells us about this issue and how to make it compatible with the ICC Statute.

The UN Charter envisioned and incorporated norms to rule a world where the use of armed force, with few exceptions, notably of self-defense and authorization by the Security Council, would be unlawful: art. 2(4) states that "All Members shall refrain in their international relations from the threat or use of force against the territorial integrity or political independence of any state or in any other manner inconsistent with the Purposes of the United Nations". This article creates a duty to refrain from the threat or use of force and, consequently, implies that there is international responsibility if the state does not comply with it. It does not address the issue of whether such responsibility is of a civil or a criminal nature. Much less does it give us clear guidance as to the type of international responsibility that would apply to the individuals who perpetrated the acts leading to aggression.

Arts. 10, 11 and 12 regulate the powers of the General Assembly to discuss and make recommendations concerning the threat or use of force, stating that this organ "may discuss any questions or any matters within the scope of the present Charter" (art. 10), "may discuss any questions relating to the maintenance of international peace and security ... and, except as provided in Article 12, may make recommendations with regard to any such questions ..." (art. 11(2)) and that "While the Security Council is exercising in respect of any dispute or situation the functions assigned to it in the present Charter, the General Assembly shall not make any recommendation with regard to that dispute or situation unless the Security Council so requests" (art. 12(1)). Therefore, these provisions assign responsibilities to the General Assembly for discussing and making recommendations concerning the maintenance of international peace and security except when the Security Council is exercising its powers concerning that dispute.

The Charter then deals with the Security Council, stating, in art. 24, that "In order to ensure prompt and effective action by the United Nations, its Members confer on the Security Council primary responsibility for the maintenance of international peace and security ..." and that "In discharging these duties the Security Council shall act in accordance with the Purposes and Principles of the United Nations. The specific powers granted to the Security Council for the discharge of these duties are laid down in Chapters VI, VII, VIII and XII." So, the Charter considers that the Security Council has primary responsibility for the maintenance of peace and security but this function is shaped as a duty, bound by the Purposes and Principles of the Organization, rather than as a power or a right.[3]

Further on, the Charter addresses this issue in Chapter VII, under the title "Action with Respect to Threats to the Peace, Breaches of the Peace, and Acts of Aggression", stating, in art. 39, that "The Security Council shall determine the existence of any threat to the peace, breach of the peace, or act of aggression and shall make recommendations, or decide what measures shall be taken in accordance with Articles 41 and 42, to maintain or restore international peace and security". So, it seems that the Charter created a duty for the Security Council to determine the existence of any act of aggression as well as the duty to either make recommendations or impose sanctions in accordance with arts. 41 and 42. This seems also to have been the conclusion reached by the International Court of Justice in its Advisory Opinion on Certain Expenses, in which it stated that it found that "under Article 24 the responsibility of the Security Council in the matter was 'primary', not exclusive and that the Charter

---

[3]   This is a position that has been sponsored by mainstream scholarship. See, for instance, Delbruck, in Simma, Bruno ed., *The Charter of the United Nations – A Commentary*, Beck, Munchen, 1994, Art. 24, page 400 and ff.: "...The SC shall act in 'accordance with the Purposes and Principles of the United Nations.' This is an indication that although the 'political approach' is intended to take priority in the actions of the organization, at least the limits of the Charter have to be observed". Addressing the issue of exclusive competence, he concludes: "In other words, placing the primary responsibility for the maintenance of peace and security on the SC means that the SC and the GA have a parallel or concurrent competence with regard to dealing with questions of the maintenance of peace, but that the SC possesses exclusive competence with regard to taking effective and binding action, especially enforcement measures.... At the same time, this interpretation of the term 'primary responsibility' does not exclude the possibility that the GA, while recognizing the primary responsibility of the SC, may become active in the field of the maintenance of peace under the general and specific powers conferred upon it, as the GA did in fact rule when it adopted the Uniting for Peace Resolution" (page 402).

made it abundantly clear that the General Assembly was also to be concerned with international peace and security".[4]

Finally, the Charter assigned functions in this area to another organ, the International Court of Justice (ICJ), with both litigious and consultative competencies. The Statute of the ICJ considers the Court competent for any legal disputes between parties which have accepted its jurisdiction, concerning: "a) the interpretation of a treaty; b) any question of international law; c) the existence of any fact which, if established, would constitute a breach of an international obligation; d) the nature or extent of the reparation to be made for the breach of an international obligation." (art. 36(2)). Furthermore, these judgments, if not complied with voluntarily, may originate an action by the Security Council, according to paragraph 2 of art. 94 of the Charter, which states: "If any party to a case fails to perform the obligations incumbent upon it under a judgment rendered by the Court, the other party may have recourse to the Security Council, which may, if it deems necessary, make recommendations or decide upon measures to be taken to give effect to the judgment". As for the consultative competence, art. 96 states that both the General Assembly and the Security Council may request an advisory opinion on any legal question and that the other organs and specialized agencies, with previous authorization by the General Assembly, may "request advisory opinions of the Court on legal questions arising within the scope of their activities".

The Charter is mute concerning international criminal responsibility of individuals and does not even address the issue of the crime of aggression, whether committed by individuals or States. However, it provides us with an organic division of tasks, stating that, besides the

---

[4] Certain Expenses of the United Nations (Article 17, Paragraph 2, of the Charter), 20 July 1962 (Case Summaries), www.icj-cij.org . Further on, the Court, addressing the issue of art. 11(2) concerning the referral of "action" to the Security Council, stated that "the action referred to in that provision was coercive or enforcement action. In this context, the word 'action' must mean such action as was solely within the province of the Security Council, namely that indicated by the title of Chapter VII of the Charter.... Accordingly, the last sentence of Article 11, paragraph 2, had no application where the necessary action was not enforcement action". Later, addressing the character of the operations in Congo, the Court considered it impossible to conclude that they affected the powers granted to the Security Council by the Charter since "these operations did not involve 'preventive or enforcement measures' against any State under Chapter VII and therefore did not constitute 'action' as that term was used in Article 11". If the large scale military operations in Congo were not considered "action", there is an almost unavoidable argument that the determination of aggression for purposes of individual criminal responsibility to be established by a judicial organ should not fall under such a category.

Security Council, the General Assembly has competencies in the maintenance of international peace and security (which it used in drafting resolution 3314 (XXIX) on the definition of aggression as recommended guidelines for the Security Council[5] and, more liberally, to adopt resolution 377(V), the Uniting for Peace resolution, to solve situations in which the Security Council could not discharge its duties) and that the ICJ has jurisdiction for deciding on any international legal question and on the existence of any fact that would constitute a breach of an international obligation (which the Court used, concerning armed force, not only in the *Nicaragua* and *Lockerbie* cases, but also in other instances, including its early opinion on the *Certain Expenses* case[6]).[7]

---

[5] Nowhere in the records of the Special Committee on the Question of Defining Aggression or on those of the 6th Committee or of the Plenary Meeting of the General Assembly which adopted the Definition of Aggression without a vote, in what would become res. 3314 (XXIX), could I find any intervention that disputed, in any way, the power of the General Assembly to define aggression.

On a related point, arising from that definition, art. 5(2) of its Annex states: "A war of aggression is a crime against international peace. Aggression gives rise to international responsibility". Some have argued that this provision applies to individual criminal responsibility, thus excluding from this crime all acts of aggression that would not amount to a "war of aggression". My opinion is that the resolution was addressing solely state criminal responsibility. The resolution was framed as a recommendation with guidelines for SC action, this latter organ lacking any powers in the Charter to decide on individual criminal responsibility and nowhere in the resolution actions of individuals being addressed. On the contrary, the resolution addresses solely state action. I believe most scholarship would agree with this interpretation: see, for instance, the categorical words of Randelzhofer on the definition of Aggression: "Moreover, Art. 5 para. 2 speaks somewhat enigmatically of 'responsibility' which, coupled with 'international', clearly relates to state rather than individual responsibility". in Simma, Bruno *op.cit.*, page 127.

[6] For the *Certain Expenses* opinion, see footnote 4. For the others, see ICJ Cases Concerning the Military and Paramilitary Activities In And Against Nicaragua (Judgment 27 June 1986) and Concerning Questions of Interpretation and Application of the 1971 Montreal Convention Arising From the Aerial Incident at Lockerbie (Judgment of 27 February 1998), both in the internet site referred to in footnote 4.

In the *Nicaragua* case, the Court stated (paras. 32-35) that although it had been suggested that the questions of use of force and collective self-defense were not justiciable, it considered that they would not lead it to overstep proper judicial bounds and that, consequently, it was equipped to determine on such issues.

[7] Professor Condorelli added a powerful argument, in his speech on the Conclusion of the present Meeting, referring to the powers that the Charter assigns, in art. 51, to each State Member of the United Nations to determine, for the purpose of self-defense, whether aggression has occurred. If this judgment lies, for certain purposes, in each State, there seems to be no scope for arguing that the Security Council is the only entity to which the Charter attributed powers for determination of aggression, whatever the purpose of those powers were.

Positions at the Preparatory Commission

Faced with this situation, the arguments and proposals in the Preparatory Commission for the International Criminal Court for harmonizing competencies concerning the crime of aggression have covered, not surprisingly, since no clear guidance is given from previous documents and practice, a wide range of positions. These positions go from the idea that the Security Council has exclusive powers to determine aggression by a State, which is a pre-condition for individual criminal responsibility for such crime, to the point of view that there is no competency in individual criminal responsibility assigned by the Charter to the Security Council and that, therefore, the conditions for the exercise of this jurisdiction lie solely in the International Criminal Court.

From my point of view, the arguments for the exclusivity of the Security Council concerning the determination of aggression for purposes of the jurisdiction of the ICC, are not convincing, since the exclusivity of the determination of the situation (and, one must add, not of the criminal responsibility, be it of a State or of an individual) lies solely in the capacity, in Chapter VII, of taking "action" through the imposition of sanctions, be they of an armed or non-armed character.[8]

One could argue, however, that, although the Charter assigns competencies in the area of the maintenance of peace and security to several organs, had it envisioned questions of criminal responsibility of States, it would have granted them to the Security Council. This argument would be coupled with the idea, put forward several times by the Security Council permanent members, that no individual criminal responsibility can originate without a previous determination that an aggression was perpetrated by a State.

I have serious doubts that such is the sole conclusion one can draw from the Charter. Although this document is silent on the matter, as we saw before, its spirit seems to point to the possibility of a judicial decision concerning criminal responsibility. In fact, the ICJ can decide on any legal question and the issue of criminal responsibility (be it of a State or of an individual) seems to be a legal rather than a political question. The Charter assigned to the Security Council the political decisions of applying sanctions whenever aggression occurred but certainly did not assign to it the determination of criminal responsibilities to a State or an individual. On

---

[8]   In the same sense, for the link between art. 39 and arts. 41 and 42 of the Charter, see the considerations by the ICJ in "Certain Expenses", reproduced in footnote 4, and its understanding of "action".

the other hand, the determination of aggression by a State as a pre-condition for its international responsibilities does not lie solely, at least, in the Security Council, as the advisory opinion of the ICJ on "Certain Expenses", the judgments on the Nicaragua and the Lockerbie cases and the pending cases of Yugoslavia against several NATO countries and of the Democratic Republic of Congo against Uganda have shown us.[9] The ICJ has never refused a case that involved the determination of the use of force based on arguments of inadmissibility of a political question and on the competencies of the Security Council, having considered that its judgments, even when they went against SC determinations, prevailed, as legal determinations, over political ones.[10]

Furthermore, practice has shown that the record of the Security Council in stating that a situation is one of aggression is, at best, sporadic: in res. 82 (V), concerning the invasion of South Korea, it considered merely that there was a "breach of peace", in the case of the invasion of East Timor, it simply requested Indonesia to withdraw its forces from the Territory without qualifying the situation (res. 384 (1975) and res. 389 (1976)), in the case of the invasion of Kuwait by Iraq, it considered, in res. 660 (1990) and ff., that there was an "invasion" and a "breach of peace and security" and only "aggressive acts" against diplomatic personnel and premises (in res. 667 (1990)) but never a situation of "aggression". It has used the expression "act of armed aggression" in res. 573(1985), concerning an Israeli raid on PLO targets in Tunisia and "acts of aggression" in res. 577 (1985) relating to the South African attacks in Angola and in very few, if any other, situations. Besides, there were, of course, several instances of serious use of armed force, notably during the cold war, that remained unmentioned since the veto power paralyzed the Council.

---

[9] Some of these cases have been mentioned in previous footnotes. For the others, see Case Concerning the Legality of the Use of Force (Yugoslavia v. several NATO members), General List No. 111, and Case Concerning Armed Activities on the Territory of the Congo (Democratic Republic of the Congo v. Uganda), General List No. 116.

[10] The *Lockerbie* case is particularly clear in the issue of the powers of the ICJ v. SC, at least once a case has began. The Court stated, in its Judgment of 27 February 1998: "Security Council resolutions 748 (1992) and 883 (1993) were in fact adopted after the filling of the Application on 3 March 1992. In accordance with its established jurisprudence, if the Court had jurisdiction on that date, it continues to do so; the subsequent coming into existence of the above-mentioned resolutions cannot affect its jurisdiction once established". Judge Kooijmans, it his Separate Opinion, makes the point even clearer, stating that "The fact that a situation has been brought to the attention of the Security Council and that the Council has taken action with regard to that situation can in no way detract from the Court's own competence and responsibility to objectively determine the existence or non-existence of a dispute".

On the other hand, the Charter does assign responsibilities to the Security Council in determining when a State has committed aggression (irrespective of whether that was a crime or not) and refers to this explicitly in art. 39. The Charter does not attribute the specific duty of determination of aggression in any other provision concerning any other organ of the U.N. system. This state of affairs seems to lend some support to those who argue that such a determination is a pre-requisite for any criminal responsibility of an individual involved in the acts that led to that aggression. Although I believe, as stated before, that other organs, namely judicial, also have powers in this area, in no case do they appear to be exclusive either. So, it does not seem to me that the argument that the Security Council plays no role in the question of aggression is a plausible one either. Art. 24 may reinforce this line of reasoning since it assigns to the Security Council "primary responsibility for the maintenance of international peace and security". Moreover, and most importantly, considerations of stability and harmony would probably lead many not to want to live in a world where international political organs, namely the Security Council, would defy judgments of international judicial institutions such as the ICC.

Harmonization of Positions

As mentioned before, it is not surprising that several interpretations of the Charter sprouted in the Preparatory Commission of the ICC. In fact, the Statute cannot go against the Charter (as referred in art. 5(2) of the Statute and as a consequence of the primacy established in art. 103 of the Charter) but the Charter does not address this issue. Interpretations have to be contextual, teleological, be based on the preparatory works or on the political and case law developments. It is not surprising that there is no consensus, then, as to the legal interpretation: the question is, fundamentally, political. I believe that one must have present that what we are seeking is not the best legal interpretation, since none will be undisputedly accepted, but a harmonization of different interpretations and a political compromise within the range of possible interpretations. We are, fundamentally, dealing with this problem for the first time in history and we are doing it in a period of transition between international models of world order.

Several proposals have been presented that try to bridge the gap between positions that defend the exclusive responsibility of the Security Council in determining aggression of a State, taken as a pre-requisite for deciding on individual criminal responsibility, and those that argue that the Security Council has no role at all in this matter, since the determination of aggression of a State is a legal question that was not assigned by the Charter to the Council.

These compromise proposals have fundamentally considered that the primary responsibility for determining State aggression lies in the Security Council but that a failure by this organ to fulfill this responsibility cannot render the jurisdiction of the ICC inoperative and nonexistent in practice: they leave to a judicial organ (the ICC, in the case of the Cameroon, Greek – Portuguese and Colombian proposals[11]) or to a mix of judicial and political organs (the ICJ and the General Assembly, in the case of the Bosnia – New Zealand – Romania proposal[12]) the determination of such a situation.

Other proposals have been hinted at or discussed in the corridors of the UN basement: they range from the possibility of a request by the General Assembly for an advisory opinion by the ICJ on the initiative of the ICC itself or of the Assembly of States Parties, to the consideration that the determination of aggression by the Security Council for the purposes of the ICC jurisdiction could be a procedural rather than a substantive issue, thus without the operation of the veto power.

It seems that there has been no lack of imagination or initiative to propose compromise models in the Preparatory Commission. However, in order to advance the work and find the political consensus that is missing, the study of substantive proposals is as important as a procedure conducive to obtaining results. The Working Group on Aggression, after a period of touching upon several issues,[13] has been concentrating on individual proposals that represent the pondering of several of the factors previously

---

[11] The proposal by Cameroon, presented in Doc. A/CONF.183/C.1/L.39, of 2 July 1998, was later reproduced in PCNICC/1999/INF/2 of 2 August 1999; the Greek – Portuguese proposal is in PCNICC/1999/WGCA/DP.1 of 7 December 1999 and was later included in PCNICC/2000/WGCA/DP.5 of 28 November 2000; the Colombian proposal can be found in PCNICC/2000/WGCA/DP.1.

[12] See U.N. Doc. PCNICC/2001/WGCA/DP.1, of 23 February 2001.

[13] The Working Group produced a "Compilation of Proposals on the Crime of Aggression submitted at the Preparatory Committee on the Establishment of an International Criminal Court (1996-1998), the United Nations Diplomatic Conference of Plenipotentiaries on the Establishment of an International Criminal Court (1998) and the Preparatory Commission for the International Criminal Court (1999)", U.N. doc. PCNICC/1999/INF/2, of 2 August 1999, a "Consolidated Text of Proposals on the Crime of Aggression", reproduced in U.N. doc. PCNICC/2000/L.4/Rev.1 of 14 December 2000, a "Preliminary List of Possible Issues Relating to the Crime of Aggression" U.N. doc. PCNICC/2000/WGCA/RT.1 of 29 March 2000, a "Reference Document on the Crime of Aggression, Prepared by the Secretariat", U.N. Doc. PCNICC/2000/WGCA/INF/1, of 27 June 2000.

debated. Although this step represents progress, there is the need for a consensual basis for work, to which the discussion can refer and build upon, to avoid the risk of successive replacement of proposals, none of which is able to gather consensus. This basis seems to be ripe as far as definition is concerned, with the use of brackets, for instance, but it is at a more underdeveloped stage regarding the conditions for exercise of the ICC jurisdiction.

We could probably think of a basis for work in this area containing three possible models: those that leave the conditions of exercise of the jurisdiction over this crime exclusively to the Security Council or to the ICC; those that leave it to the ICC in case of a lack of determination by the Security Council within a certain period; and those that involve other organs in the process, such as the General Assembly or the Assembly of States Parties and the ICJ. This new basis of work would not prejudge any position but it would clarify and organize the debate and would contribute to its successful outcome. As always, procedure is fundamental and, many times more decisive than substance in achieving results.

We are building a new institution that will have, for the first time since the creation of the United Nations, jurisdiction over individuals for the crime of aggression and the U.N. Charter did not foresee it when it was drafted. Legal guidance is, therefore, at most partial and a political compromise through a structured and clear debate seems to be the only way to successfully discharge the mandate in our hands.

14. The ICC and the Security Council: About the Argument of Politicization

MARJA LEHTO[*]

We have heard a number of very stimulating presentations on the subject of the relationship between the ICC and the Security Council, and have considerable food for thought and debate already. On my part I will not comment on the various proposals and will not advocate any of them – as Professor Politi has said, the magic formula still remains to be found. As I will cover much of the same ground as previous conference speakers, I will try to be as brief and concise as possible.

I would like to bring the question back to the alleged politicisation of the Court, should it venture to consider a complaint of aggression without a prior determination of an act of aggression by the Security Council. Warning about the risks of politicizing the ICC has been a powerful argument in the debates of the Preparatory Commission – but also an intriguing one.

The argument has been raised in support of a clear division of labour between the ICC and the Security Council, namely that the Court would only consider the question of individual criminal responsibility while the question of State responsibility for an act of aggression would be left to the Security Council. A consequential conclusion is that the investigation and prosecution of a crime of aggression by the Court would depend on a prior determination by the Security Council that an act of aggression has occurred. Whether this should be so or whether the Court should be allowed to proceed on its own has been disputed mainly with regard to situations where the Council's determination does not exist and is not forthcoming.

[*] Ministry of Foreign Affairs, Helsinki.

What is meant by politicization? Let me illustrate the argument by quoting one of the most prominent interventions in favour of it: "... to ask the Court in the absence of a determination by the Security Council to decide that an act of aggression has taken place would (…) endanger (…) its judicial role and image. (...) Imagine the immense difficulties that the ICC, as a court of law, would face in dealing even with relatively simple acts of aggression. (...) is it equipped to consider such matters as historical claims to territory, maritime boundaries, legitimate self-defence under Article 51 or legitimate reprisals? (...) And is the competence of the Court, in any event, not limited to jurisdiction over natural persons? (...) we must not turn the ICC into a political forum discussing the legality of use of force by States."[1]

The essence of the politicization argument is thus a concern about a confusion of mandates; a concern about the judicial role and integrity of the ICC; about an encroachment by the Court on the responsibilities of the Security Council – and finally about a necessary distinction between the legal and political spheres. Determining that an act of aggression has taken place is said to lie outside the scope of the judicial function. At the same time, there are many who see that the politicization argument would only apply to the ICC, and not to the International Court of Justice – a useful distinction that leaves room for innovative mechanisms to allow the ICC to use its particular jurisdiction also in the absence of a Security Council determination.

Let us look at these problems more closely. In what follows I will suggest that there may, in fact, be some legitimate overlap between the political and the judicial functions – certainly not to the extent that the two would or should be melting together, but rather in the sense of suggesting that the boundaries between the different functions are less clear and categorical than what the argument of politicization seems to convey.

It is clear that the Security Council has different functions from those of a Court of Law. The process in the Security Council is very different from judicial proceedings. The Council is a political organ with wide discretionary powers. Its determination under Article 39 that an act of aggression has taken place is not automatic but a result of political considerations. Nor is the Council bound to make such a determination - it can always choose inaction. And indeed, as has been pointed out by Professor Gaja, the Security Council has so far preferred to use the

---

concepts of threat against the peace or breach of the peace as a basis for actions under Article 39 of the Charter. It has been frequently underlined in the Preparatory Commission that this fact should not be seen as a failure on the part of the Council but rather as considered use of the options provided by the Charter.

Quoting Judge Schwebel who wrote in his dissenting opinion to the *Nicaragua* case, in 1984, "the Security Council may take legal considerations into account but unlike a court, is not bound to apply them".[2] While this continues to be a highly relevant remark, one must notice a significant development in the practice and policy of the Security Council over the past ten or twelve years. The role of the Security Council has become increasingly central in the enforcement of international legal norms. The Council has not only, increasingly, taken into account legal considerations but has also made legal determinations, sometimes of a type "that is in the heart of what is normally seen as judicial activity. (...) Determinations of international law are now part and parcel of decision-making on collective measures".[3] So much so that it has become customary to speak of the quasi-judicial role of the Security Council. The expansion to the legal realm has been coupled with a change in the Council's agenda, a growing sensitivity for issues like international crimes, protection of civilians, and international humanitarian law.

Have there been similar changes with regard to the judicial function? According to the famous dictum of the International Court of Justice, "The Council has functions of a political nature assigned to it, whereas the Court exercises purely judicial functions".[4] From this statement that seems to emphasize the division of labour between the two organs, the Court concludes that both "can therefore perform their separate but complementary functions with respect to the same events".[5] The ICJ itself has never refused to deal with a case on the basis that the dispute at hand would not be justiciable. It has been able to handle very political questions, often ones involving use of armed force, without compromising its judicial integrity. Examples include the often-cited *Nicaragua* and *Lockerbie* cases (not to mention the advisory opinion on nuclear weapons) as well as several decisions related to various ongoing conflicts.

---

[2] *Nicaragua* case, ICJ Reports 1986, p. 290.
[3] Rosalyn Higgins, *Problems and Process*, Oxford University Press 1994, p. 182.
[4] *Nicaragua* case, ICJ Reports 1986, p. 435.
[5] *Ibid.*

The case of the ICC is certainly different in that it will have jurisdiction over individuals, not over States and should therefore rather be compared with the international war crimes Tribunals. Reference is often made in this context to the Yugoslavia Tribunal's decision in the *Tadić* case. When considering the distinction between international and internal conflict, the Tribunal did not hesitate to make determinations on the basis of general rules of State responsibility. It may be that the ICTY should rather have asked the Security Council to seek an advisory opinion on the question from the ICJ, as the President of the ICJ has suggested.[6] Notwithstanding the importance of ensuring legal coherence, as underlined by Judge Guillaume, one could also argue that such determinations were within the implied or inherent powers of the Tribunal. Action which promotes the effectiveness of an international organization in carrying out its given function is in general considered to be within the competence of the organization as long as it is not expressly excluded in its constituent instrument.[7] And, certainly, there is no provision on applicable law in the Statute of the ICTY.

The ICTY treated the question of the nature of the conflict – internal or international – as a preliminary question that had to be settled for the purposes of establishing individual criminal responsibility in the case at hand. That was probably not a unique situation. One could well assume that similar preliminary questions are bound to emerge, from time to time, when the future ICC deals with complex situations referred to it. As Victoria Hallum has pointed out, some war crimes may be of the same complexity as the crime of aggression. One could hold that the power to deal with such questions is inherent to the function of an international court endowed with jurisdiction over the most serious international crimes – provided, of course, that the provisions of the Statute do not preclude such a possibility. The provisions on applicable law and on the qualifications of judges, for instance, do not seem to do so.

The conclusion in relation to the crime of aggression is that the Court would in principle be able to make preliminary determinations pertaining to State responsibility without overstepping the proper judicial grounds – and without being politicized.

I am not saying that this would be an advisable outcome – or a probable one in terms of where we stand in our negotiations, but I share the view that there are different options available in purely legal terms. How the provision on the preconditions to the jurisdiction of the Court will be

---

[6]   Speech to the Sixth Committee of the U.N. General Assembly on 27 October, 2000.

[7]   Dapo Akande, *The competence of international organizations and the advisory jurisdiction of the International Court of Justice*, EJIL 9 (1998), p. 446.

formulated, will depend on the political choices of the future Review Conference. The Conference may, if it so wishes, opt for an express exclusion and decide that a prior determination of the Security Council of an act of aggression is always a prerequisite for the Court to deal with a complaint related to a crime of aggression. No doubt there are many possible reasons why this should be so, but I will not dwell on them since that is not my topic. I will mention only one such reason, namely the close and complex relationship between the two institutions. The Court is already integrated in the system of common security by virtue of articles 13(b) and 16 of the Statute.

Rather than a question of principle, the argument of politicization highlights a very practical problem. In the long term the Court will need the support of or at least a benevolent attitude on the part of the Security Council. This is why the Review Conference, eventually, may choose to avoid an in-built conflict in the relationship between the ICC and the Security Council – especially if the Security Council on its part is willing, as would be fitting to its new humanitarian vocation, to take action to ensure the effective and impartial prosecution of the crime of aggression.

15. Conclusions Générales

LUIGI CONDORELLI[*]

1. Introduction

Les organisateurs de ce colloque, mes chers amis Mauro Politi et Giuseppe Nesi, m'ont prié juste au début de nos travaux de tirer quelques conclusions à l'issue des trois jours de débats. J'ai bien entendu accepté (comment aurais-je pu leur dire non?), mais à une condition: de pouvoir m'exprimer en français, langue dans laquelle je suis – bien davantage qu'en anglais – à l'aise pour "improviser". De plus, je me sens engagé à l'instar des vrais francophones dans la défense du rôle international de cette belle langue qui constitue mon outil de travail quotidien depuis tant d'années...

L'écrasante majorité des intervenants pendant nos séances était formée de personnes pourvues d'une grande expertise en la matière, du fait d'être parmi les protagonistes principaux des négociations en cours concernant l'agression comme crime relevant de la compétence de la C.P.I. Ce n'est pas mon cas: je suis, quant à moi, un spectateur. Très intéressé certes, mais spectateur. Ceci constitue évidemment un désavantage important, puisque j'ignore beaucoup des tenants et aboutissants d'un débat très complexe, voire souvent confus, même s'il est vrai que les riches propos que j'ai entendus trois jours durant ont pas mal comblé mes lacunes de connaissance. J'ai cependant un grand avantage dont je vais profiter (et, si j'en suis capable, vous faire profiter): celui d'être "irresponsable". Je veux dire par là que, n'ayant présentement ni n'ayant eu par le passé aucun rôle à jouer en tant que représentant de tel ou tel gouvernement dans les pourparlers internationaux pertinents, je jouis d'une liberté totale par rapport aux divers intérêts qui influencent les positions des Etats sur un thème politiquement – c'est indéniable – des plus délicats. Mes commentaires, en somme, expriment les réactions d'un universitaire "pur", qui observe et analyse un débat fort stimulant avec un regard totalement dépourvu de conditionnements et préjugés politiques; ou tout au moins

---

[*] Professor of International Law, University of Geneva.

dépourvu de conditionnements et préjugés de source autre que son propre entendement. Il se peut que ce regard extérieur soit utile pour votre réflexion à venir.

Mes remarques vont s'ordonner en deux parties.

Dans la première je vais essayer d'identifier ce qui, concernant le crime d'agression, est déjà acquis et tranché dans le Statut de Rome: ce qui, en somme, représentera en quelque sorte la *lex lata* dès que le Statut sera entré en vigueur. Cette entrée en vigueur ne va bien entendu pas le rendre intouchable, cela va de soi; mais il s'agirait alors, justement, de modifier la *lex lata*, de changer des engagements déjà pris par les Etats parties.

Dans la deuxième partie de mes conclusions, en revanche, je mettrai en évidence ce qui reste à décider, afin de contribuer à déterminer la latitude des choix encore à faire. Elle est grande, c'est hors de doute, mais elle est tout de même circonscrite par une double série de facteurs: d'une part, par ce qui a déjà été décidé préalablement dans le Statut; d'autre part, par tout ce qui relève des principes indérogeables du droit international. Il convient d'assimiler à ceux-ci les principes de la Charte des N.U., et non seulement à cause de la prévision explicite en ce sens que proclame le deuxième paragraphe de l'art. 5.

2. Première partie: questions déjà tranchées par le Statut de la C.P.I.

Si l'on étudie de près le Statut de Rome, on s'aperçoit aisément qu'au sujet du crime d'agression un certain nombre de questions ont déjà été réglées de manière telle qu'un retour en arrière apparaît maintenant fort difficile.

La première est de toute évidence la qualification de l'agression comme l'un des "...crimes les plus graves qui touchent l'ensemble de la communauté internationale", ainsi que le proclame le 4ème Considérant du Préambule et le réitère le premier paragraphe de l'art. 5. Cette qualification a deux corollaires évidents, dont il convient de souligner l'importance: d'abord celui d'après lequel l'agression est à considérer, de par sa gravité même, comme rentrant nécessairement dans le noyau dur des crimes tombant dans la sphère de compétence de la Cour (voire auxquels la compétence de la Cour est "limitée", ainsi que l'indique la première phrase de l'art. 5). On pourrait dire, en somme, que le Statut condamne les négociateurs que vous êtes à réussir dans la tâche de mettre au point une définition appropriée du crime d'agression, afin qu'il devienne possible pour la Cour d'exercer une fonction dont il est déjà acquis qu'elle lui appartient *de jure*. Quant à l'autre corollaire, il s'agit de constater le déclenchement, pour l'agression aussi, du "...devoir de chaque Etat de soumettre à sa juridiction criminelle les responsables..." (Préambule, 6ème Considérant): sans doute pas tout de suite, mais certainement dès que la définition sera adoptée conformément aux modalités fixées à l'art. 5, paragraphe 2, les Etats devront donc prévoir au niveau de leurs droits internes la responsabilité pénale individuelle pour les auteurs d'actes d'agression et édicter les mesures nécessaires pour que leurs juges puissent les réprimer à l'enseigne du principe d'universalité de la juridiction.

Ce crime d'agression, cependant, malgré l'accord existant quant à sa gravité, devra être défini ultérieurement ; et malgré que le principe de la compétence de la Cour à son égard soit acquis, les conditions d'exercice d'une telle compétence restent à fixer, ainsi que l'indique explicitement le $2^{\text{ème}}$ paragraphe de l'art. 5. L'acceptation de ce texte a des implications évidentes: elle exprime *a contrario* l'adhésion générale à l'idée que le droit international en vigueur ne dispose pas encore d'une définition satisfaisante et opérationnelle du crime individuel d'agression, ou tout au moins ne dispose pas d'une définition suffisamment complète (et en règle avec le principe de légalité) qui pourrait être utilisée *hic et nunc* par le juge international. Il en va de même évidemment pour le juge interne et pour l'obligation des Etats de mettre en œuvre la répression à l'échelle nationale, comme je viens de le signaler.

Troisième point: tant la définition du crime individuel d'agression, que la fixation des conditions d'exercice de la compétence de la C.P.I. à son sujet, devront être en harmonie avec la Charte des N.U. Certes, cette indication explicite que souligne l'art. 5 peut apparaître redondante et, donc, superflue, aucun traité international ne pouvant prescrire des obligations en contradiction avec celles découlant de la Charte (art. 103). Il ne convient toutefois pas de la prendre à la légère: elle témoigne, en effet, de la reconnaissance générale qu'il y a bien un problème très délicat qu'il faudra régler à l'avenir sans apporter des entorses à la Charte. L'art. 5 met ainsi indirectement en exergue le nœud fondamental à trancher par les négociations futures: celui de savoir comment se raccordent les compétences de la Cour en matière de crime individuel d'agression à celles du Conseil de sécurité relatives à l'agression aux termes de la Charte, c'est-à-dire dans les relations interétatiques.

Dernier point: les régimes juridiques prévus aux articles 11 et 12 sont pertinents "à l'égard des crimes visés à l'article 5", donc de toute évidence à l'égard de l'agression aussi. Il faut en déduire que, quand le crime d'agression sera défini, la C.P.I. devra pouvoir exercer ses compétences au sujet de celui-ci de la même manière que pour le génocide, les crimes contre l'humanité et les crimes de guerre. Autrement dit, la procédure pourra être déclenchée par un Etat partie, par le procureur ou par le Conseil de sécurité; toutefois la Cour, si elle est saisie par un Etat ou par le procureur, ne pourra procéder qu'à condition que l'Etat sur le territoire duquel le crime a eu lieu ou l'Etat national de l'accusé aient accepté sa compétence, alors qu'une telle condition n'est pas de mise en cas de saisine par le Conseil de sécurité. Il est vrai que l'art. 5, 2ème paragraphe, réserve la possibilité que des conditions spécifiques d'exercice par la C.P.I. de ses compétences, concernant l'agression, soient fixées ultérieurement. Cependant, ces conditions supplémentaires ne devraient pas pouvoir altérer l'architecture générale du système, telle que les articles 11 et 12 la dessinent en proclamant explicitement sa pertinence – on l'a dit – pour tous les crimes visés à l'art. 5.

Dans son rapport, Giorgio Gaja a présenté une analyse différente en se basant sur la teneur d'une autre disposition du Statut, l'art. 121 (relatif aux amendements), à laquelle l'art. 5, 2ème paragraphe, fait renvoi pour déterminer par quelles procédures devront être réalisées la définition du crime d'agression et la fixation des conditions d'exercice de la compétence de la Cour à son égard. Un tel renvoi impliquerait que ladite définition serait à concevoir comme équivalant à un amendement. Or, le paragraphe 5 de l'article 121, en envisageant la possibilité d'un amendement aux articles 5 à 8 du Statut, établit que, lorsqu'un tel amendement entrera en vigueur, la Cour ne pourra pas exercer sa compétence à l'égard d'un crime qui en ferait l'objet si "… ce crime a été commis par un ressortissant d'un Etat partie qui n'a pas accepté l'amendement ou sur le territoire de cet Etat". Au vu de cette formulation, il semblerait alors que, pour que la Cour puisse procéder en cas d'agression, l'"amendement" doit lier tant l'Etat national du criminel présumé que l'Etat sur le territoire duquel le crime aurait été commis, alors que cette double condition – on le sait – n'est pas requise par le Statut pour les crimes figurant aux articles 5 à 8 actuels. De plus, il faudrait déduire du libellé négatif et absolu de la disposition en question qu'aucune exception ne jouerait non plus en cas de saisine de la Cour par le Conseil de sécurité, toujours en matière d'agression : ici aussi la double condition serait exigée.

A mon avis, la lecture que Giorgio Gaja fait de l'art. 121, paragraphe 5, est correcte (sous réserve de la question portant sur la saisine de la Cour par le Conseil de sécurité) en ce qui concerne les "amendements" proprement dits aux articles 5 à 8 du Statut, entendus au sens d'adjonctions de nouvelles *figurae criminis* (ou en tout cas de modifications des dispositions qui les composent actuellement). Par contre, il me semble qu'elle ne saurait être jugée comme pertinente s'agissant, non pas de modifier l'art. 5 en l'amendant, mais de le compléter pour ce qui est d'un crime, l'agression, qui figure déjà nommément dans la liste, quoique sans définition précise; un crime qui, du fait même d'être listé, tombe pleinement dans la sphère d'action des articles 11 et 12, dont on a souligné l'indication explicite suivant laquelle leur régime juridique est applicable "à l'égard des crimes visées à l'art. 5", sans exception. La thèse critiquée produirait, en somme, une contradiction irréconciliable entre diverses dispositions du Statut, qui peut être évitée par l'interprétation proposée. Celle-ci, de surcroît, écarte l'absurdité de créer un obstacle (représenté par la double condition déjà citée) pour la saisine de la Cour par le Conseil de sécurité juste en matière d'agression, alors qu'un tel obstacle ne joue pas pour tous les autres crimes figurant aux articles 5 à 8 du Statut. Il va de soi, en effet, que c'est spécialement face à l'agression que le Conseil de sécurité doit pouvoir agir "en vertu du Chapitre VII de la Charte" (art. 13, b, du Statut de Rome), en utilisant le cas échéant la C.P.I., sans être conditionné par le fait que celle-ci soit acceptée ou non par tel ou tel Etat. En somme, c'est pour assurer le plein respect des fonctions du Conseil de sécurité face aux situations relevant du Chapitre VII, telles que consacrées par la Charte, que l'art. 13, b, permet au Conseil d'actionner la Cour sans se soumettre aux conditions requises pour sa saisine par un Etat ou par le Procureur; il serait donc totalement incohérent qu'un tel affranchissement ne soit pas de mise en cas d'agression.

Il est vrai qu'à l'art. 5, deuxième paragraphe, il est question de l'adoption des dispositions relatives à la définition de l'agression, ainsi qu'à la fixation des conditions d'exercice par la Cour de ses compétences en la matière, "conformément aux articles 121 et 123". Cependant, l'utilisation dans ces buts de la procédure relative aux amendements et à la révision du Statut n'implique pas que l'on doive traiter comme un amendement à l'art.

5 une intervention normative que l'article en question envisage et préconise lui-même, et qui ne sera donc nullement destinée à l'"amender" ou modifier, mais, au contraire, à le concrétiser et finaliser. Autrement dit, il est évident que l'on devra faire application, alors, de tout ce qui sera applicable de l'art. 121, mais pas de son paragraphe 5.

3. Deuxième partie : remarques sur les choix qui restent à faire

Venons-en maintenant aux questions qui ont été davantage débattues, portant sur les nœuds les plus délicats qui restent à trancher dans les négociations à venir. Mes observations ont pour but principal de mettre en évidence quels sont les conditionnements réels qui pèsent sur les négociateurs, et en particulier les limites à ne pas franchir, afin que la future définition du crime d'agression et des conditions d'exercice de la compétence de la C.P.I. à son égard soit, non seulement respectueuse des principes fondamentaux du droit international et de ceux de la Charte des N.U., mais également cohérente avec eux.

Ici aussi je partagerai mes propos en deux parties (ou sous-parties) : d'abord (sous *a*) je discuterai de certains aspects relatifs à la définition, puis (sous *b*) des conditions d'exercice de la compétence de la Cour concernant l'agression, en centrant le regard sur les futures relations entre le juge international pénal et le Conseil de sécurité.

a) Quelques problèmes de définition du crime d'agression

La première observation à faire concerne un point qui semble acquis, et qui a d'ailleurs été présenté comme tel dans nos débats: c'est l'idée d'après laquelle l'accusation portée contre un individu d'être l'auteur d'un crime d'agression présupposerait nécessairement l'existence d'un Etat agresseur. C'est une conception qui m'apparaît, quant à moi, très discutable: je ne vois pas, en effet, pourquoi il devrait être *a priori* exclu que l'on puisse criminaliser comme auteurs d'agressions des particuliers n'agissant pas pour le compte d'Etats, mais plaçant leur action dans le cadre de puissants groupes non-étatiques, comme des multinationales du crime organisé, des mafias, des armées privées, des cartels de la drogue ou des centrales terroristes. Que l'on puisse ou non parler d'"agression" au sens "inter-étatique" de la Charte lors d'attaques d'envergure venant de telles organisations si aucun Etat n'est derrière elles, il n'en reste pas moins qu'il ne serait pas du tout choquant d'imaginer que de telles attaques soient qualifiées de "crimes d'agression" sur le plan de la responsabilité pénale individuelle.[1]

Deuxième remarque: il a été dit et répété que ce crime est nécessairement un *"leadership crime"*, dont ne peuvent se rendre responsables que des personnes au sommet de la hiérarchie du pouvoir à l'intérieur d'un Etat, disposant de ce fait de la capacité de décider le lancement d'une agression. Cette vision, s'il fallait l'entendre en ce sens que finalement seul un dictateur absolu pourrait être un agresseur, et donc soumis à la répression internationale, serait à mon sens quelque peu naïve: on ne saurait exclure d'emblée, me semble-t-il, des hypothèses d'agressions étant le fruit de décisions collectives, prises par tout un appareil dirigeant d'un Etat (y compris un gouvernement, une majorité parlementaire, la direction des partis au pouvoir, etc.).

Laissant de côté ces aspects, je conviens quant à l'idée que pour parvenir à la définition du crime d'agression on peut de toute façon prendre appui sur un noyau d'éléments mis à disposition par la pratique internationale, tant sur le versant de la notion d'agression "interétatique" que connaît la Charte, que sur celui du crime engendrant la responsabilité pénale individuelle (je me réfère, bien entendu, spécialement aux statuts des Tribunaux militaires internationaux de Nuremberg et de Tokyo). Il va de soi, cependant, que certaines notions doivent être mises à jour en tenant compte des développements récents du droit international. Ainsi, par exemple, il ne serait plus approprié de discuter en termes de crime consistant dans le fait de lancer une "guerre" d'agression : il peut, en effet, y avoir agression indépendamment du fait de savoir si, techniquement, il s'agit d'une guerre ou non, le déclenchement d'un "conflit armé" devant être considéré comme suffisant.

Quant aux liens entre les deux versants à peine évoqués, j'ai déjà signalé pourquoi à mon sens un crime individuel d'agression peut être conçu sans qu'il soit indispensable d'identifier préalablement un Etat agresseur. La réciproque, par contre, est bien difficile à concevoir, en ce sens que, si il y a un Etat agresseur, il doit nécessairement y avoir alors,

---

[1] Le bien-fondé de cette remarque, que j'avais présentée lors du Colloque de Trento, est évidemment confirmé de manière éclatante par les événements du 11 septembre 2001 et par certaines réactions de la communauté internationale à leur égard … .

derrière le "voile corporatif", des individus criminels: à savoir, les décideurs de cet Etat. Si ceci est exact, il s'ensuit alors que la définition de l'agression dans les relations d'Etat à Etat, telle que la connaissent les principes de la Charte, doit inévitablement influencer de manière directe la définition de l'agression comme crime individuel. On sait à ce sujet que tout emploi de la force dans les relations entre Etats n'est pas qualifiable d'agression, si un niveau suffisant de gravité n'est pas atteint, ainsi que l'indique explicitement la Rés. 3314/74 de l'A.G. et le confirme la C.I.J. (en son arrêt de 1986 dans l'affaire du Nicaragua). Mais pour le reste, il serait me semble-t-il difficile, voire impossible, de prétendre de manière rationnelle et crédible que l'une ou l'autre des hypothèses d'agression identifiées dans la liste figurant dans ladite résolution pourrait ne pas impliquer la responsabilité pénale individuelle des gouvernants de l'Etat agresseur. Il va de soi qu'il ne s'agit pas seulement de mettre en évidence l'absurdité – qui saute littéralement aux yeux – de propositions ultra-restrictives, comme celle suggérant de définir le crime d'agression en se référant aux seuls cas d'annexion ou d'occupation par la force de territoires d'autres Etats (qui impliquerait, par exemple, que la destruction de villes par des bombardements aériens à tapis ne serait pas un comportement agressif...). Il convient, en fait, d'insister sur ce point plus général: s'il y a agression interétatique, quelles qu'en soient les modalités, il doit y avoir alors un ou plusieurs décideurs à qualifier de criminels.

Face aux difficultés de parvenir à une définition analytique largement partagée, certains ont fait valoir pendant le débat qu'une définition flexible et générale du crime d'agression, laissant un "degree of discretion" à la C.P.I., pourrait représenter une sorte de solution de compromis, peut-être acceptable pour tous. Je dois avouer que je n'y crois pas. A part d'inévitables objections – plus ou moins fondées au demeurant – basées sur le principe de légalité, une telle solution suppose un haut degré de confiance dans la Cour dont je ne vois pointer à l'horizon aucun signe révélateur. Bien au contraire, il me semble que l'ensemble des négociations passées et présentes au sujet de la C.P.I. laissent transparaître clairement des préoccupations et des craintes très répandues quant à une Cour qui, profitant d'espaces trop vastes laissés à son appréciation, élargirait progressivement son mandat par voie d'interprétations audacieuses et innovatives (comme l'a fait, on le sait, le "Tribunal Cassese"). Ce que j'ose appeler un "reflex anti-Cassese" contribue à mon sens considérablement à expliquer pourquoi le Statut de Rome est si détaillé, restrictif et précautionneux dans la définition des crimes (et des "éléments des crimes") soumis à la compétence de la Cour, et pourquoi les listes de crimes qui étaient "ouvertes" dans les Statuts des TPI pour l'ex-Yougoslavie et le Rwanda sont devenues exhaustives dans le Statut de Rome.

b) Des conditions d'exercice de la compétence de la Cour découlant des compétences du Conseil de sécurité ?

Il va de soi que la question de loin la plus discutée, tant ici, pendant nos journées de colloque, que dans les diverses enceintes internationales actives sur ces thèmes, reste celle de savoir comment doivent s'articuler et s'ordonner les compétences de la C.P.I. en matière de crimes d'agression, par rapport à celles du Conseil de sécurité. Celui-ci, en effet, dans le cadre de sa "responsabilité principale" du maintien de la paix, se voit confier par le Chapitre VII de la Charte une sorte de véritable monopole opérationnel en fait de mesures concrètes de sécurité collective à mener face à un acte "interétatique" d'agression. Auraient-ils alors raison, ceux qui considèrent que la Cour ne doit pas pouvoir juger un individu prétendument auteur d'un crime d'agression si le Conseil n'a pas préalablement constaté qu'une agression a bien eu lieu dans les relations internationales? Ou bien faut-il estimer que les compétences d'un organe judiciaire ne doivent subir aucun conditionnement au moyen de décisions d'un organe politique, comme il arriverait inévitablement si l'on accordait une sorte de primauté au Conseil?

Les intérêts de haute politique qui alimentent les différentes thèses en présence sont trop connus pour qu'il soit nécessaire de les rappeler maintenant. Aux fins des présentes conclusions, il n'est d'ailleurs pas vraiment utile d'exprimer des positions militantes, inévitablement à caractère politique, en faveur de l'une ou de l'autre. Il convient par contre de se pencher sur l'argument juridique fondamental dont on prétend qu'il fonderait la primauté du Conseil sur la Cour, pour en vérifier la consistance. Reconstruisons donc, d'abord, ce que je n'hésite pas à appeler le pseudo-raisonnement proposé par les partisans de la primauté, puis déconstruisons-le (voire démystifions-le) en mettant en évidence ce qui en fausse chaque passage.

Fondamentalement, le raisonnement en question base sa conclusion sur deux prémisses. Première prémisse: on ne saurait prétendre qu'un individu est l'auteur d'un crime d'agression s'il n'y a pas un Etat qualifiable d'agresseur. Deuxième prémisse: d'après la Charte des N.U., un Etat ne peut être qualifié d'agresseur si le Conseil de sécurité ne l'a pas constaté en exerçant le pouvoir que lui octroie en exclusivité l'art. 39 de la même Charte. Conclusion: *ergo*, sans la constatation préalable, effectuée par le Conseil de sécurité, de l'agression, la Cour ne saurait être investie de la répression du crime d'agression.

La déconstruction de ce faux syllogisme est facile, puisque chacune des deux prémisses sur lesquelles il se base est inexacte. Pour ce qui est de la première, j'ai déjà remarqué auparavant que le crime (individuel) d'agression est parfaitement concevable dans certains cas d'actions de particuliers ne pouvant pas être attribuées à des Etats: je n'entends pas revenir sur ce point à nouveau. Mais c'est surtout la deuxième prémisse qui est totalement boiteuse, étant le fruit d'une lecture très approximative et partielle de la Charte des N.U.

Il n'est absolument pas vrai, en effet, que la Charte accorde un monopole au Conseil de sécurité en matière de constatation de l'agression. Ce qui est exact est que les mesures de sécurité collective prévues au Chapitre VII peuvent être adoptées par le Conseil exclusivement si celui-ci a préalablement constaté qu'on est bien en présence d'une menace à la paix, d'une rupture de la paix ou d'un acte d'agression. Ceci implique alors que, quand le Conseil, en se basant sur l'art. 41 de la Charte, voudra saisir la C.P.I. face à "… une situation dans laquelle un ou plusieurs … crimes … (d'agression) paraissent avoir été commis …" (pour reprendre la terminologie de l'art. 13, b, du Statut de Rome), il devra en principe avoir d'abord constaté qu'il y a bien eu une agression au sens de la Charte, étant donné le lien déjà explicité qui rattache normalement l'agression "interétatique" au crime individuel d'agression. Aucun monopole, cependant: tant que les mécanismes de la sécurité collective n'ont pas – ou pas encore – été mis en branle par le Conseil de sécurité, la Charte prévoit expressément que les Etats, dans le cadre de leur droit "naturel" ou "inhérent" de légitime défense individuelle et collective, sont appelés à évaluer eux-mêmes s'il y a ou non une agression dont ils seraient les victimes. Il est alors parfaitement logique d'imaginer un système dans lequel, indépendamment de toute intervention du Conseil de sécurité et sans que soient d'aucune façon contredits les principes fondamentaux de la Charte, ces Etats jouiraient de la possibilité de saisir la Cour en lui soumettant eux-mêmes la situation les concernant, dans laquelle un ou plusieurs crimes individuels d'agression paraissent avoir été commis.

Ce n'est pas tout, d'ailleurs: il convient, en effet, de ne pas oublier l'Assemblée générale et sa compétence – justement générale – pour ce qui est de "discuter toutes questions se rattachant au maintien de la paix et de la sécurité internationales" (art. 11, paragraphe 2, de la Charte). Le fait que le mot "agression" ne figure pas dans cette disposition n'exclut de toute évidence pas que – tout en respectant les compétences du Conseil de sécurité – l'Assemblée générale soit habilitée à constater elle aussi l'existence d'une agression, à en débattre et à faire des recommandations à ce sujet aux Etats et/ou au Conseil. Le crime individuel d'agression étant un des "crimes d'une telle gravité... (qui) ...menacent la paix, la sécurité et le bien-être du monde" (3ème Considérant du Préambule du Statut de Rome), et sa répression relevant donc des mesures de maintien et rétablissement de la paix et de la sécurité internationales, il s'ensuit que l'Assemblée générale doit pouvoir s'intéresser d'une telle répression. A défaut d'habilitation à saisir directement la C.P.I. (sauf, pourquoi pas, en sollicitant l'action du Procureur, dans le cadre des relations à établir entre les organes de la C.P.I. et des organisations intergouvernementales, auxquelles diverses dispositions du Statut de Rome font allusion), l'Assemblée pourrait sans aucun doute faire aux Etats intéressés et au Conseil des recommandations, y compris celle de déclencher la procédure devant la Cour en déférant au procureur des situations dans lesquelles des crimes d'agression paraissent avoir été commis.

De toute façon, les compétences du Conseil de sécurité et celles de la Cour porteront sur des objets reliés, mais distincts (l'existence d'une agression interétatique pour le premier, la responsabilité pénale individuelle en matière de crime d'agression pour la seconde), de sorte que de véritables conflits entre les résultats de leur exercice respectif sont très improbables et, à la limite, d'une gravité bien réduite, vu l'étendue fort circonscrite de l'effet de la chose jugée qui se rattacherait en tout état de cause à une condamnation ou à un acquittement prononcés par la C.P.I.

4. Conclusion

Mes conclusions sont les suivantes.

Malgré que le Statut de la C.P.I. renvoie à plus tard la définition du crime d'agression et la fixation des conditions d'exercice de la compétence de la Cour à son égard, un certain nombre de questions sur ces sujets sont en réalité déjà réglées aujourd'hui: autrement dit, les décisions futures représenteront des sortes de tesselles venant compléter une mosaïque déjà bien avancée, quant à son état de finition, même en matière d'agression.

Quant aux choix qui restent à faire, il sont certes nombreux et importants, il faut le reconnaître. Toutefois, il convient d'insister sur un point: il n'est absolument pas vrai que les futures dispositions sur le crime d'agression, pour être compatibles avec la Charte, devront sauvegarder un prétendu monopole du Conseil de sécurité en matière de constatation de l'agression. La Charte ne prévoit ni n'exige rien de pareil. Certes, la Charte n'interdit pas non plus qu'une subordination de la C.P.I. au Conseil soit créée à l'avenir: une telle solution pourrait donc bien être choisie à l'issue des négociations, si les membres permanents du Conseil de sécurité parvenaient à convaincre un nombre suffisant de délégations que leurs intérêts personnels correspondent à l'intérêt général. Mais il faut d'avance mettre au clair qu'une telle solution serait déterminée, alors, par des choix et des équilibres purement politiques, et non pas imposée par la Charte.

AFTERWORD

THE INTERNATIONAL CRIMINAL COURT AND THE CRIME OF AGGRESSION: FROM THE PREPARATORY COMMISSION TO THE ASSEMBLY OF STATES PARTIES AND BEYOND

16. An Outsider's View

GIUSEPPE NESI*

1.

There were several reasons for organizing a second Trento meeting on the International Criminal Court (ICC), dedicated to the crime of aggression.[1] In spring 2001 the negotiations on the crime of aggression had reached a crossroad after the first seven meetings of the Preparatory Commission for the International Criminal Court (PrepCom) and before the final rush toward the entry into force of the Rome Statute and the setting up of the ICC. Furthermore, after the lengthy discussions in the PrepCom on the definition of the crime of aggression and the conditions for the exercise of the Court's jurisdiction, there was a general perception that the time was ripe for an open and even outspoken debate in an "unorthodox" atmosphere. By gathering in an academic environment, protagonists of the negotiations and eminent legal scholars hoped they could cast some light on one of the most complex and politically sensitive issues left open by the Rome Statute. The University of Trento, with the support of the Autonomous Province of Trento, generously provided just such a venue.

The general expectations were satisfied by three days of intense discussions. Diplomats, scholars and students joined together in a new exercise, on an informal basis, that reconfirmed the potential of the Trento University and the entire Trentino – Alto Adige Südtirol as the ideal venue for discussions of topics concerning international law and relations among States.

Expectations were high that the outcome of the Trento meeting would encourage the taking of other steps during the eight session of the PrepCom in New York from 24 September to 5 October 2001.

The tragic events of September 11, 2001 had a shocking impact on the United Nations even jeopardizing the opening of the fifty-sixth Session of the General Assembly. Nevertheless, the eighth session of the PrepCom

---

* Professor of International Law, University of Trento.
[1] As recalled in the preface of the present volume, the first Trento meeting on the ICC took place in May 1999. The Proceedings of the 1999 Trento Meeting were published in: Politi and Nesi (eds.), *The Rome Statute of the International Criminal Court. A Challenge to Impunity*, Ashgate, Aldershot, 2001.

took place as scheduled. Those who were present in New York on that occasion realized that there would also be huge setbacks in the negotiations on the crime of aggression and the ICC because of those events.

Meanwhile, there was a rapid increase in the number of States to ratify the Rome Statute; during the ninth session of the PrepCom in April 2002, the sixtieth ratification was deposited, allowing the Statute to enter into force on 1 July 2002, at the beginning of the tenth and last PrepCom session.

During those days, the Proceedings of the 2001 Trento meeting were almost ready for the press; publication was delayed, however, to include an account of the negotiations on the crime of aggression that took place at the First Meeting of the Assembly of the States Parties in September 2002.

At the time of the Trento meeting, in deference to the guest speakers, I refrained from delivering a paper. In the following pages I will summarize the works of the PrepCom from September 2001 to July 2002 and the decisions of the first session of Assembly of States Parties on the issue of the crime of aggression.[2] My summary will be complemented by a paper from Silvia Fernández de Gurmendi, the coordinator of the Working Group on Aggression of the PrepCom.

2.

Despite the initial setbacks, almost one month before the beginning of the eight session, a twofold proposal was presented by Bosnia and Herzegovina, New Zealand, and Romania dealing with the definition of the crime of aggression and the conditions for the exercise of jurisdiction over such a crime (PCNICC/2001/WGCA/DP.2/ and Add. 1). The same States had tabled an earlier version of the same at the seventh session of the PrepCom (PCNICC/2001/WGCA/DP.1) and discussed it during the Trento Meeting. The proposal raises different hypotheses:

a) if a situation involving aggression is referred to the ICC by the Security Council under art. 13 (b) of the Statute, there is a presumption of the existence of the crime of aggression since the Security Council, acting on

---

[2]   Before going to the press with the present paper, an article dealing also with the works of the PrepCom on the crime of aggression and the ICC was published, giving an interesting reconstruction of the sessions: Trahan, J., *Defining "Aggression": Why the Preparatory Commission for the International Criminal Court Has Faced Such a Conundrum*, 24 *Loyola of Los Angeles International and Comparative Law Review*, August 2002, 439-473.

the basis of art. 39 of the U.N. Charter, should have based its referral on the existence of such crime (para. 2 of the proposal).

b) If the referral is made by a State party or results from investigations initiated *proprio motu* by the Prosecutor, the ICC should ascertain whether the Security Council, acting under art. 39, assessed the existence of an act of aggression (para. 3 of the proposal).

The ICC's inquiries into the Security Council determination of the existence of an act of aggression could lead to different outcomes: if the determination is in the affirmative, the Prosecutor has no further obstacle to proceeding with the investigation and prosecution if he/she so decides. If, on the contrary, the Security Council denies the existence of any act of aggression, the ICC will no longer deal with the case. If, finally, no determination on the part of the Security Council is made, the Court should notify the Security Council of the situation before the Court in order to seek a determination by the Security Council, according to art. 39 of the Charter (para. 4 of the proposal).

The great novelty of this proposal is the mechanism introduced for the case in which the Security Council does not make any determination under article 39 or invoke article 16 of the Statute (i.e., deferral of the matter for a period of 12 months). In such a case the Court may request the General Assembly to seek an advisory opinion of the International Court of Justice (article 96 of Charter of the U.N. and article 65 of the Statute of the ICJ) on the legal question of whether or not aggression has been committed by the State concerned (para. 5 of the proposal). If the ICJ advisory opinion declares that there has been aggression, the ICC can proceed (para. 6 of the proposal).

The proposal on the definition of the crime of aggression presented by Bosnia and Herzegovina, New Zealand, and Romania, tried to make a clear-cut distinction between the concept of the *crime of aggression* – which could give rise to individual criminal responsibility – and the concept of *aggression by a State* (PCNICC/2001/WGCA/DP.2). The commentary to this proposal specifies that even if article 5, para. 2 of the Rome Statute requires that only the crime of aggression be defined,

> Because aggression by a State is a precondition to the prosecution of an individual for the crime, it is necessary to make clear in the Statute itself what type of action on the part of a State will trigger individual criminal responsibility and open the way to a prosecution in the International Criminal Court.

Recalling the definition inscribed by the International Law Commission in its draft Code of Crimes against the Peace and Security of Mankind (1996), and thus on the provisions of the Nuremberg and Tokyo Statutes, the crime of aggression is defined as a crime committed by a person who, "being in a position to exercise control over or direct the political or military action of a State, intentionally and knowingly orders or participates actively in the planning, preparation, initiation or waging of aggression committed by that State". It is thus clear that the crime of aggression is intended to be a "leadership crime"; only those who are in a particular position within the State can actually plan, prepare, initiate or wage acts of aggression. Furthermore, the act must be committed "intentionally and knowingly", i.e., the perpetrator must be well aware of the type of act he/she has set in motion.

Finally, as regards the concept of aggression committed by a State, para. 2 of the proposal stated that it means, "The use of armed force to attack the territorial integrity or political independence of another State in violation of the Charter of the United Nations". The first part of para. 2 specifies that this definition is made, "For the purposes of the exercise of jurisdiction by the Court over the crime of aggression". It attempts to draw a distinction between State conduct that may constitute a violation of article 2, para. 4 of the Charter of the United Nations (and so give rise to international responsibility) and State conduct that is sufficiently serious in nature to require the individual responsible to be held accountable in a criminal court.

The proposal presented by Bosnia and Herzegovina, New Zealand and Romania was discussed during the eighth PrepCom and compared to proposals made in previous sessions. The debate was accelerated by the decision of the Coordinator of the Working Group on the crime of aggression, the Argentinian diplomat Silvia Fernández de Gurmendi, to prepare, after the eighth session of the PrepCom, a "consolidated text of proposals on the crime of aggression" that reflected all the proposals thus far presented on both the definition of aggression and the conditions for the exercise of jurisdiction over that crime (PCNICC/2001/L.3/Rev. 1, Annex 3). A preliminary list of possible issues relating to the crime of aggression was inserted in the same document.

3.

On the basis of this document, the debate on the crime of aggression was expected to resume during the ninth session of the PrepCom, on 8-19 April

2002.[3] On the eve of the ninth session of the PrepCom, on 1 April 2002, a discussion paper proposed by the coordinator was presented (PCNICC/2002/WGCA/RT.1) that summarized the proposals concerning both the definition of the crime of aggression and the conditions for the exercise of jurisdiction. In an attempt to streamline the work of the delegates, the document defined the act of aggression committed by a State by referring to the UNGA Resolution 3314 (XXIX) of 14 December 1974, subject to a prior determination of the Security Council (para. 1). Para. 2 of that document reaffirms that "a crime of aggression means an act committed by a person who, being in a position to exercise control over or direct the political or military action of a State, intentionally and knowingly orders or participates actively in the planning, preparation, initiation or waging of an act of aggression". It goes on to indicate three different options. According to the first option, such an act of aggression would amount, "by its characteristics and gravity, to a war of aggression". The second option referred to an act of aggression as being "the object or result of establishing a military occupation of, or annexing, the territory of another State or part thereof". According to the third option, the act of aggression would be "in manifest violation of the Charter of the United Nations".

The last two paragraphs of the discussion paper proposed by the coordinator dealt, respectively, with the case where the Prosecutor intends to proceed with an investigation into a crime of aggression (para. 3), and with the case where the Security Council does not make a determination as to existence of an act of aggression or invoke article 16 of the Statute within six months of the date of notification (para. 4). In the former case, it is provided that it is up to the Court to ascertain whether the Security Council has made a determination that a State committed an act of aggression that meets the definition provided by the first paragraph of the proposed provision. Paragraph 3 provides that "If no Security Council determination exists, the Court shall notify the Security Council of the situation before the Court so that the Security Council may take action, as appropriate under article 39 of the Charter of the United Nations". According to paragraph 4, when the Security Council does not make a determination of the existence of an act of aggression or invoke article 16 of the Statute within six months of the date of notification, the ICC has four options:

---

[3] Meanwhile, in January 2002, the U.N. Secretariat issued two interesting documents (PCNICC/2002/WGCA/L.1 and PCNICC/2002/WGCA/L.1/Add.1) giving a historic review of developments relating to aggression. They are available on line at the U.N. website.

1) to proceed with the case;
2) to dismiss the case;
3) to request the General Assembly to make a recommendation within 12 months. In the absence of such a recommendation, the Court may proceed with the case;
4) to request the General Assembly to seek an advisory opinion from the International Court of Justice (article 96 of the U.N. Charter and article 65 of the ICJ Statute) on whether or not an act of aggression has been committed. According to this last option, the ICC may proceed with the case if the ICJ gives an advisory opinion that an act of aggression has been committed by the State concerned or makes a finding, in proceedings brought under Chapter II of its Statute, that an act of aggression has been committed by the State concerned.

The discussion paper received little support from the majority of PrepCom delegates. Their main concern was that the various proposals had been "oversimplified" since they felt that the proposed options for the crime of aggression could not be reconciled. The same could be said for the determination of the conditions for the exercise of jurisdiction over an act of aggression. In other words, in an attempt to find a common ground, the text paradoxically ascertained the enormous distances between the various proposals thus far presented. According to many delegates it was unclear why the definition of the act of aggression, taken from UNGA Res. 3314 (XXIX), had to be "subject to a prior determination by the United Nations Security Council" (para. 1) while the determination of the conditions for the exercise of jurisdiction over that act was left to different procedures in para. 4. Para. 2 gave three different options on the "substance" of the crime of aggression, ranging from a very narrow case ("by its characteristics and gravity amounts to a *war of aggression*") to a very broad one ("is in manifest violation of the Charter of the United Nations"), with an intermediate hypothesis ("has the object or result of establishing a military occupation of, or annexing, the territory of a State or a part thereof").

The debate on the crime of aggression during the ninth PrepCom session was therefore fruitless, leaving the impression that no progress has been made over time and the discussions were back to where they started.[4]

---

[4]   The impression was confirmed by informal proposals presented by Samoa, France, Cameroon, and The Netherlands.

4.

The entry into force of the Rome Statute was celebrated on 1 July 2002, at the opening of the tenth and last session of the PrepCom. During the same period the new born Statute had to face the first serious difficult test of its functioning.[5]

The participating States had to address new proposals presented by several delegations.[6] One of the most interesting was from the Delegation of Samoa (PCNICC/2003/WG CA/DP.2, 21 June 2002). It explained that while the PrepCom was focusing its efforts on the definition of aggression and the conditions under which the ICC should exercise its jurisdiction, the "question of the Elements (of the crime of aggression) should not pass entirely unnoticed with the impending demise of the Preparatory Commission". In the Samoan Delegation's views the issue of the Elements of that crime was important "not only for its own sake, but also, and perhaps more importantly, for the light that it might shed on the technical aspects of the *definition* and *conditions*". On this basis, Samoa thought that the "conceptual structure" contained in articles 30 and 32 of the Rome Statute should be applied to the paper proposed by the coordinator on 1 April 2002 (PCNICC/2002/WGCA/RT.1).

The Samoan proposal is complex and deserves an in-depth study that falls outside the scope of the present paper. Suffice it to say that its complexities and the late stage of its presentation probably contributed to the lack of development during the last session of the PrepCom. Nonetheless, the Samoan proposal will most likely be resumed and debated in an appropriate manner at forthcoming meetings on the topic of aggression.

---

[5] Reference is here to the adoption by the Security Council of Resolution 1422 (2002) of 12 July 2002, according to which the Security Council, "acting under Chapter VII of the Charter of the United Nations, requests, consistent with the provisions of Article 16 of the Rome Statute, that the ICC, if case arises involving current or former officials or personnel from a contributing State not a Party to the Rome Statute over acts or omissions relating to a United Nations established or authorized operation, shall for a twelve-month period starting 1 July 2002 not commence or proceed with investigation or prosecution of any such case, unless the Security Council decides otherwise".

[6] We refer to the proposal presented by the Netherlands (PCNICC/2002/WGCA/DP.1), Samoa (PCNICC/2002/WGCA/DP.2), Colombia (PCNICC/2002/WGCA/DP.3), the Movement of Non-Aligned Countries (PCNICC/2002/WGCA/DP.4), Belgium, Cambodia, Sierra Leone, and Thailand (PCNICC/2002/WGCA/DP.5).

5.

At the close of the substantive debate of the PrepCom's last session various informal proposals were made on the follow-up to the negotiations on the issues related to the crime of aggression.

One of them maintained that it would be worthwhile to cease debate on the issue for a time, deferring further decisions to the Assembly of States Parties (ASP) but without soliciting indications from the PrepCom. Accepting this proposal would have amounted to putting the delicate issue "on ice" for several years.

A second proposal was to assign to the Sixth Committee of General Assembly the task of elaborating both the definition of the crime of aggression and the conditions under which the ICC could exercise its jurisdiction over this crime. This proposal was also rejected because the Sixth Committee had tried unsuccessfully several times in the past to define the crime of aggression.

A third proposal aimed to create an open-ended working group on the crime of aggression: such a proposal would have allowed U.N. Member States that were not parties to the Rome Statute to participate in the negotiations.

The latter proposal was accepted. The resolution adopted by the ASP provides for the establishment of "a special working group on the crime of aggression, open on an equal footing to all UN Member States or members of specialized agencies or of the International Atomic Agency, to draft proposals for a provision on aggression in accordance with paragraph 2 of article 5 of the Statute and paragraph 7 of Resolution F adopted by the United Nations Conference of Plenipotentiaries on the Establishment of an International Criminal Court on 17 July 1998".[7] The special working group thereby established "shall submit such proposals to the Assembly for its consideration at a Review Conference, with a view to arriving at an acceptable provision on the crime of aggression for inclusion in the Statute in accordance with the relevant provisions of the Statute".[8]

---

[7]   Resolution F of the Final Act of the Rome Conference stated: "7. The Commission shall prepare proposals for a provision on aggression, including the definition and Elements of Crimes of aggression and the conditions under which the International Criminal Court shall exercise its jurisdiction with regard to this crime. The Commission shall submit such proposals to the Assembly of States Parties at a Review Conference, with a view to arriving at an acceptable provision on the crime of aggression for inclusion in this Statute. The provisions relating to the crime of aggression shall enter into force for the States Parties in accordance with the relevant provisions of this Statute".

[8]   These are the words used in PCNICC/2002/2/Add. 2, p. 2.

On 7 February 2003, the Assembly decided, on the basis of the proposal of the Bureau, that the Special Working Group on the Crime of Aggression should meet during annual sessions of the Assembly of States Parties. Thus, the first meeting would be held at the second session of the Assembly, in September 2003.[9]

The forthcoming works on the ICC and the crime of aggression will therefore be open to all U.N. Member States and not only to the States Parties to the Rome Statute. This decision confirms, once again, that the States Parties to the Rome Statute are ready to make every possible effort to urge all the States that are not parties to join the membership of the Statute for the sake of achieving its universality.

In conclusion, after four years of negotiations at the PrepCom on the definition of aggression and the conditions under which the ICC has jurisdiction, one can still ask whether it was wise to include the crime of aggression in the Rome Statute without providing a clear definition. One can also ask whether this inclusion was a concession by States that did not intend to ratify the Statute or a real achievement by the majority of the world community which genuinely believes that the goals of the Rome Statute can be achieved.

The Special Working Group now has a heavy burden. The summary of the last sessions of the PrepCom gives the impression that there were some positive developments and probably a moment in which States were very close to their aim. They must now avoid falling into the trap of Penelope, undoing by night what they have achieved by day.

---

[9] ICC-ASP/1/L.5, ASP report adopted by consensus on 23 April 2003. The resolution continues: "In addition, the Assembly, on the basis of the report of the Bureau, took note of the idea of holding informal inter-sessional meetings of the Special Working Group, but decided that it was not in a position to make any recommendations, since some delegations might find it financially difficult to send representatives to inter-sessional meetings and it would thus be preferable that the Special Working Group meet during the annual sessions of the Assembly of States Parties. The door was left open, however, for any Government wishing to fund the holding of an inter-sessional meeting".

17. An Insider's View

SILVIA A. FERNÁNDEZ DE GURMENDI*

Introduction

The International Law Commission (ILC) included aggression in its draft Statute for an International Criminal Court but, as was the case for the other crimes, did not provide a definition.[1] In the commentary to the draft, the ILC acknowledged the special problem that was raised by this crime in that there was no treaty definition comparable to genocide.[2] Furthermore General Assembly Resolution 3314 of December 14, 1974 dealt with aggression by States, not with the crimes of individuals, and was designed as a guide for the Security Council not as a definition for judicial use.[3] But, the ILC concluded:

> [G]iven the provisions of Article 2(4) of the Charter of the United Nations, that resolution offers some guidance, and a court must, today, be in a better position to define the customary law crime of aggression than was the Nuremberg Tribunal in 1946. It would thus seem retrogressive to exclude individual criminal responsibility for aggression (in particular, acts directly associated with the waging of a war of aggression) 50 years after Nuremberg[4].

* Diplomat. Legal Adviser of the Permanent Mission of Argentina to the United Nations. Coordinator of the Working Group on Aggression of the Preparatory Commission for the International Criminal Court.
[1] Report of the International Law Commission on the Work of its Forty-sixth Session, Draft Statute for an International Criminal Court, U.N. GAOR, 49th Sess., Supp. No. 10, at 70, art. 20 (b), U.N. Doc. A/49/10 (1994) [hereinafter Draft ILC Statute]
[2] See *ivi*, at 72, para. 6.
[3] See Definition of Aggression, G.A. Res. 3314 (XXIX), U.N. GAOR, 6th Comm.,29th Sess, 2319th plen. mtg. (1974).
[4] Draft ILC Statute, *supra* note 2, at 72, para. 6.

During the negotiations of the Rome Statute many delegations quoted this ILC statement and shared the historical assessment of the Commission; that it would be retrogressive to exclude individual criminal responsibility for aggression 50 years after Nuremberg. Unfortunately, however, the negotiations of the International Criminal Court demonstrated that the international community was not in a better position to define the crime and all efforts to that effect failed in the Rome Diplomatic Conference.[5]

At the end of the Rome Conference, after extensive discussions, proponents and opponents of the inclusion of aggression within the jurisdiction of the International Criminal Court had to admit that negotiations had ended in a tie and accepted a codified impasse. Aggression was indeed included but without immediate effect due to a provision stating that:

> The Court shall exercise jurisdiction over the crime of aggression once a provision is adopted in accordance with articles 121 and 123 defining the crime and setting out the conditions under which the Court shall exercise jurisdiction with respect to this crime. Such a provision shall be consistent with the relevant provisions of the Charter of the United Nations.[6]

As part of the compromise, the Preparatory Commission of the International Criminal Court created at the end of the Conference in order to draft supplementary instruments of the Statute, was also mandated to continue to deal with aggression. To that end, Resolution F adopted at the Conference on July 17, 1998 stated that:

> The Commission shall prepare proposals for a provision on aggression, including the definition and Elements of Crimes of aggression and the conditions under which the International Criminal Court shall exercise its jurisdiction with regard to this crime. The Commission shall submit such proposals to the Assembly of States Parties at a Review Conference, with a view to arriving at an acceptable provision on the crime of aggression for inclusion in this Statute. The provisions relating to the crime of aggression

---

[5]   For a story of the negotiations at the Rome Conference, see Herman von Hebel & Darryl Robinson, "Crimes Within the Jurisdiction of the Court", in Roy S. Lee (ed.) *The International Criminal Court: The Making of the Rome Statute, Issues, Negotiations, Results*, Kluwer Law International, The Hague, London, Boston, 1999, 79-127.

[6]   Article 5, para. 2 of the Rome Statute.

shall enter into force for the States Parties in accordance with the relevant provisions of this Statute.[7]

In fulfillment of this mandate, the Preparatory Commission established a Working Group on aggression to deal with the matter. This Working Group ended together with the Preparatory Commission in 2002 but its tasks and duties will continue to be performed by an open ended Working Group of the Assembly of States Parties.[8]

Definition of Aggression

The Working Group on aggression of the Preparatory Commission tackled both main issues referred to in article 5 of the Rome Statute and Resolution F, namely the definition of the crime and the conditions of exercise of jurisdiction by the Court.

The Precedents

Proposals introduced by delegations drew inspiration from existing precedents, namely the Charter of the International Military Tribunal of Nuremberg[9] and General Assembly Resolution 3314.[10]

Article 6 (a) of the Charter of the Nuremberg Tribunal provided for the individual criminal responsibility for crimes against peace:

> namely, planning, preparation, initiation or waging of a war of aggression, or a war in violation of international treaties, agreements or assurances, or

> participation in a common plan or conspiracy for the accomplishment of any of the foregoing.[11]

---

[7] Final Act of the United Nations Diplomatic Conference of Plenipotentiaries on the Establishment of an International Criminal Court, Res. F, para. 7, U.N. Doc. A/CONF.183/10 (1998).
[8] See Resolution ICC-ASP/1/Res.1. Continuity of work in respect of the crime of aggression. Assembly of States Parties to the Rome Statute of the International Criminal Court. First Session. New York, 3-10 September 2002. Official Records.
[9] Charter of the International Military Tribunal, 8 August 1945, available at www. Yale.edu/lawweb/Avalon/imt/proc/imtconst.htm.
[10] *Supra*, note 4.
[11] Charter, *supra* note 11, art. 6(a).

On the basis of this provision, the Tribunal proclaimed in its judgment:

> ...To initiate a war of aggression, therefore, is not only an international crime; it is the supreme international crime differing only from other crimes in that it contains within itself the accumulated evil of the whole.[12]

Efforts to sanction the crime on aggression were increased by the International Military Tribunal for the Far East ("Tokyo Tribunal"), which focused predominantly on the prosecution of perpetrators of the crime against peace. The Tokyo Tribunal relied heavily on the Pact of Paris of 1928 for the legal basis for the crime against peace. Among the separate and dissenting opinion, Judges Roling of the Netherlands and Pal from India objected that aggression had not been defined yet as a crime under international law for the purposes of ensuring individual criminal responsibility.[13] Both made a call to the international community to take the necessary legal measures in the future, in light of the horrors of the Second World War.[14]

The efforts towards this end started immediately after the war in 1946. On December 11, 1946, the General Assembly of the United Nations adopted three Resolutions. By the first one, the General Assembly established the Committee on the Progressive Development of International Law and its Codification.[15] By the second one, it directed the Committee:

> To treat as a matter of primary importance plans for the formulation, in the context of a general codification of offences against the peace and security of mankind, or of an International Criminal Code, of the principles recognized in the Charter of the Nuremberg Tribunal and in the judgment of the Tribunal.[16]

---

[12] Judicial Decisions, International Military Tribunal (Nuremberg), Judgment and Sentences, Oct.1, 1946, 41 A.J.I.L, 172, 186 (1947)

[13] See the Tokyo Judgment, Volume II, Extracts of Opinion of Mr. Justice Roling and Mr. Justice Pal (B.V.A. Roling & C.F. Ruter eds, 1977) reprinted in 1 Benjamin Ferencz, *An International Criminal Court, A Step Towards World Peace: A Documentary History and Analysis* 506 (1980), at 80-83.

[14] *Ibid.* at 507-38.

[15] Progressive Development of International Law and Codification, G.A. Res. 94 (I), U.N. GAOR, 1st Sess., 55th plen.mtg.(1946). A year later this Committee was transformed into the International Law Commission pursuant to General Assembly Resolution 174 (II) of 21 November 1947.

[16] Affirmation of the Principles of International Law recognized by the Charter of the Nuremberg Tribunal, G.A. Res. 95 (I), U.N. GAOR, 1st Sess., 55th plen. mtg. (1946).

The third resolution affirmed that genocide was a crime under international law and asked the Economic and Social Council to *"undertake the necessary studies, with a view to drawing up a draft convention on the crime of genocide".*[17]

Regarding the first two resolutions, the ILC met for the first time in 1949. On its agenda was, *inter alia*, the draft Code of Offences Against the Peace and Security of Mankind – including the formulation of the Nuremberg principles. On the basis of the reports of the Special Rapporteur, the Commission at its second session, in 1950, adopted a formulation of the principles of international law recognized in the Charter of the Nuremberg Tribunal and in the Judgment of the Tribunal and submitted these principles to the General Assembly. In 1954, it submitted a draft Code of Offences against the Peace and Security to the General Assembly. The General Assembly, considering that the draft Code of Offences against the Peace and Security of Mankind as formulated by the Commission raised problems closely related to those of the definition of aggression and also considering that the General Assembly had entrusted a Special Committee with the task of preparing a report on a draft definition of aggression, decided to postpone consideration of the draft code until the Special Committee had submitted its report.

Discussions of the definition of aggression lingered on at successive Special Committees for twenty years. Finally, by resolution 3314 (XXIX) of 14 December 1974, the General Assembly managed to adopt by consensus a Definition of Aggression.[18] Article 1 contains a generic provision, partially drawn from article 2(4) of the Charter, which stipulates that:

> Aggression is the use of armed force by a State against the sovereignty, territorial integrity or political independence of another State, or in any other matter inconsistent with the Charter of the United Nations, as set out in this Definition

---

[17] The Crime of Genocide, G.A. Res. 96 (I), U.N. GAOR, 1st Sess. 55th plen. mtg. (1946).
[18] *Supra* note 4.

Article 2 stipulates that "[t]he first use of armed force by a State in contravention of the Charter shall constitute *prima facie* evidence of an act of aggression although the Security Council ... may conclude that a determination that an act of aggression has been committed would not be justified in the light of other relevant circumstances".

In article 3 of the Definition, a number of acts that constitute aggression are enumerated. However, this list is not exhaustive, the Security Council is not bound by it, and the Security Council may also consider any other act as an act of aggression under the provisions of the Charter.

Finally, article 5, paragraph 2, stipulates that: "A war of aggression is a crime against international peace. Aggression gives rise to international responsibility".

The Negotiations at the Preparatory Commission.

Taking into account the precedents, numerous proposals were introduced at the Preparatory Commission. The results of early discussions are reflected in the consolidated text that was produced by the first coordinator of the Working Group on aggression[19] at the third session of the Prepcom in 1999.[20] Additional proposals and working documents were presented thereafter by individual delegations that fueled the debate and helped the Working Group to make progress in the understanding of the problems.

"Generic" vs. "list" approach   During the debates, there were two main schools of thought: the "generic approach" that promoted a general or abstract definition of the crime of aggression and the "list approach" which enumerated the specific acts constituting aggression.

Under the generic approach, there was a proposal to follow the Nuremberg Charter closely in that it criminalized a "war of aggression".[21] Its proponents underlined the importance of the Nuremberg Charter, which they consider to be the only authoritative text in international law, being the only one that established and actually recognized individual criminal responsibility. Against this definition, it was argued that the concept of

---

[19]   Tuvaku Manongi from Tanzania.

[20]   See U.N. Doc. PCNICC/1999/L.5/Rev.1 (Dec.22, 1999).

[21]   This proposal stated "For the purposes of the present Statute and subject to prior determination by the United Nations Security Council of an act of aggression by the State concerned, the crime of aggression means any of the following acts: planning, preparing, initiating, carrying out a war of aggression". See Consolidated Texts of Proposals on the crime of aggression prepared by the coordinator as Option 2, *supra* note 21.

"war of aggression" related to World War II and did not apply to most forms of contemporary violence. From a more technical point of view, there were objections that this definition was in fact a circular definition, a "non definition", that could hardly satisfy today's more stringent standards of legality. Consequently, within the same generic approach, other proposals contemplated definitions that drew their inspiration from Article 1 of Resolution 3314 and Article 2(4) of the U.N. Charter in order to expand the concept of the definition to other types of illicit uses of force.[22]

Opposing or supplementing the generic approach, other delegations insisted on the need of having a definition that would enumerate the list of acts constituting aggression.[23] This list, they claimed, should reproduce the one contained in Resolution 3314 which was adopted by consensus after many years of extensive negotiations and reflected customary law. Those who objected to the list maintained, however, that this Resolution was aimed at acts of States and not crimes by individuals. This was, they argued, demonstrated not only by the legislative history, but by the text of the resolution itself, including article 5 paragraph 2, of the Resolution, which seemed to draw a distinction between the war of aggression qualified as a *"crime against international peace"* and the act of aggression which *"gives rise to international responsibility"*.

Crime of aggression vs. act of aggression Regardless of the approach taken, there was a common understanding that finding a solution to the problem required taking into account two different types of responsibilities, that of the State for the commission of an act of aggression and the responsibility of an individual for committing the crime of aggression. Drawing on this common understanding, a proposal was introduced at the final stages of the negotiations at the Preparatory Commission that distinguished both concepts in the definition itself. The proposal contained two paragraphs; one defining the act of aggression and the other defining

---

[22] See, e.g. Consolidated Text by Coordinator, supra note 22, Option 1. Option 1 states: "For the purposes of the present Statute, [and subject to the determination of the Security Council regarding the act of a State,] the crime of aggression means [the use of armed force, including the initiation thereof, by an individual who is in a position of exercising control or directing the political or military action of a State, against the sovereignty, territorial integrity or political independence of a State in violation of the Charter of the United Nations]"(brackets in the original).

[23] See id. Option 1, Variation 3.

the crime, both for the purposes of the Rome Statute.[24] This proposal was welcomed by many as an important step forward, at least from a methodological point of view.

The "threshold" Despite the fundamental disagreement among delegations surrounding the definition, there was a general recognition that in order to fall under the definition of aggression, the use of force should be of certain magnitude or gravity. Uses of force of lesser magnitude such as border skirmishes, cross-border artillery, armed incursions, and similar situations could not fall under the definition of aggression. It was argued in this connection that, on one hand, the Charter itself did not consider any act of force contrary to its provision as an act of aggression. On the other hand, acts of force of lesser gravity would not fall within the jurisdiction of the ICC, which only applied to the *"most serious crimes of concern to the international community as a whole"*.[25] Consequently, delegations increasingly focused on the issue of the "threshold" or, in other words, the scale, the magnitude, or gravity required for an act of use of force to amount to aggression. Several formulations were proposed in this respect. Some delegations suggested that the threshold requirement could be created by qualifying the violation of the norm (e.g. use of force in "manifest" violation of the U.N. Charter).[26] Others suggested qualifying the acts by their consequences or goals (e.g. only acts of force that have the object of or result in an annexation or occupation of territories would be covered.[27] Finally, some delegations referred back to the Nuremberg Charter, arguing that the concept of "war of aggression" was to be used precisely because it had already a threshold built in the concept that indicated the scale of violence that was required.

---

[24] Proposal Submitted by Bosnia and Herzegovina, New Zealand and Romania, Definition for the crime of aggression, U.N. Doc. PCNICC/2001/WGCA/DP.2 (Aug.27, 2001) . The definition is divided as follows: "A person commits the crime of aggression who, being in a position to exercise control over or direct the political or military action of a State, intentionally and knowingly orders or participates actively in the planning, preparation, initiation or waging of aggression committed by that State.
For the purposes of the exercise of jurisdiction by the Court over the crime of aggression under the Statute, aggression committed by a State means the use of armed force to attack the territorial integrity or political independence of another State in violation of the Charter of the United Nations".
[25] Preamble of the Rome Statute.
[26] See Consolidated Text by coordinator, *supra* note 22, Option 1, Variation 2.
[27] See *ibidem*.

The Conditions of Exercise of Jurisdiction by the Court

Although it is not expressly said in article 5 of the Rome Statute, it is clear that the conditions of exercise of jurisdiction require discussing the links, if any, between the Court and the Security Council. The articulation of an adequate relationship with the Security Council was one of the most sensitive issues during the drafting of the Rome Statute. The relevant provisions, in particular article 16 of the Statute, continue to elicit controversy and criticism today.[28] The choice of an elliptical construction in Article 5 to describe the problem with regard to aggression, shows in itself the degree of disagreement that existed on this matter at the end of the Diplomatic Conference. For those who opposed recognizing any role of the Security Council, any express mention to the Council in Article 5 would have been unacceptable. Therefore, Article 5 only refers to the need for: "setting out the conditions under which the Court shall exercise jurisdiction with respect to this crime. Such provisions shall be consistent with the relevant provisions of the Charter of the United Nations".[29]

Quite obviously, all delegations agreed that the conditions of exercise of jurisdiction by the Court had to be consistent with the Charter of the United Nations. But the interpretations of the Charter varied dramatically and its provisions were invoked to sustain opposite views.

On one hand there were those who asserted that the Security Council had the exclusive power to determine an act of aggression by a State, which in their view, was an indispensable precondition for the determination of individual criminal responsibility by the Court.[30] This position was mainly based on Article 39 of the U.N. Charter, which assigns responsibilities to the Security Council in determining when a State had committed aggression. This position was also held by the ILC, which considered that the Security Council's special responsibilities under Chapter VII of the Charter, meant "that special provision should be made to ensure that prosecutions are brought for aggression only the Security Council first determines that the State in question has committed

---

[28] For a discussion of the role of the Security Council, see Lionel Yee, The International Criminal Court and the Security Council: Articles 13 (b) and 16, in *The International Criminal Court: The Making of the Rome Statute, Issues, Negotiations, Results*, Roy Lee ed. 1999., 143-52, *supra* note 6.

[29] Article 5, para 2.

[30] See Consolidated Text by Coordinator, *supra* note 22, Option 1, 3.

aggression in circumstances involving the crime of aggression which is the subject of the charge".[31]

The ILC Draft Statute contained a provision to that effect stating: "A complaint of or directly related to an act of aggression may not be brought under this Statute unless the Security Council has first determined that a State has committed the act of aggression which is the subject of the complaint".[32]

The exclusivity of the Security Council to determine an act of aggression was contested by those who underlined the fact that the U.N. Charter also assigned competence in the area of the maintenance of peace and security to several organs. They added that the Security Council's exclusivity lay solely in the capacity of taking "action" through the imposition of sanctions, be they of an armed or non-armed character. Finally, they argued that the Security Council had no role at all in this matter since their competencies related exclusively to States and not to individual criminal responsibility, and because the determination of aggression of a State was a legal question that was assigned to the Council by the U.N Charter only for the purposes of applying sanctions. There was, they concluded, no competence on individual criminal responsibility assigned to the Security Council by the Charter and therefore, the conditions for the exercise of this jurisdiction lay solely in the ICC. From a more pragmatic perspective they emphasized that practice had shown that the record of the Security Council in stating that a situation was one of aggression was, at best, sporadic. The Security Council, they argued, had shown over the years its resistance to determine the existence of an act of aggression for several reasons, including the paralyzing effect of the veto power of the permanent members. They concluded that the Security Council had no role in the determination of individual criminal responsibility or at best only primary, but not exclusive, competence in this field as expressly stated in Article 24 of the Charter. From a practical perspective they insisted that a failure of this organ to fulfill its responsibility could not render the jurisdiction of the ICC inoperative and nonexistent in practice.

The view that the Security Council had a primary, but not exclusive, role in the matter prompted several proposals which shared a common point of departure but contained radically different solutions to the problem. Most of these proposals seemed to accept at least two premises. Firstly, a determination of an act of aggression was a precondition for the Court to exercise its functions over the crime of aggression. Secondly, the

---

[31] Draft Statute, *supra* note 2, at 72.
[32] *Ivi*, p. 84.

Security Council had the right to be the organ that would act in the first place, providing for other alternatives only as a remedy when the Council failed to act after a certain period of time or did not use the faculty already recognized in Article 16 of the Statute to suspend proceedings by the Court.

As to the remedies for the Security Council inaction, the proposals provided for a range of options leaving the determination of an act of aggression either to the International Criminal Court itself, [33] to the General Assembly[34] or to a mix of judicial and political organs, namely the General Assembly and the International Court of Justice acting within its consultative jurisdiction.[35]

The Discussion Paper Prepared by the Coordinator

Discussions on aggression represented an enormous challenge for delegations at the Preparatory Commission both in terms of substance and diplomacy. Mistrust of each other's intentions and good faith permeated the debates and was not conducive to creating a friendly atmosphere necessary to allow progress. As a corollary, some opposed any real effort in terms of drafting as they viewed drafting as a way of prematurely imposing trends and ideas that while having important support were not yet capable of achieving consensus.

Consequently, at the early stages of the negotiations the coordinator of the Working Group could only produce a Consolidated Text of Proposals[36] which tried to compile all views which were reflected in several options containing numerous variations and numerous brackets. This text was first introduced in 1999 and was later successively reproduced in the summary proceedings of each session of the Preparatory Commission although it was in practice superseded by additional national proposals.

Eventually, debates became more technical in nature and the atmosphere evolved to a constructive one similar to the one prevailing in other groups of the Preparatory Commission. This allowed for a new attempt to focus the debate through a negotiating paper which I first

---

[33] See Consolidated Text by coordinator, *supra* note 22, Option 1, Variation 1, and Option 2.

[34] See *id.* Option 1, Variation 2.

[35] See Bosnia and Herzegovina, New Zealand and Romania proposal, *supra* note 25.

[36] See *supra* note 22.

produced in April 2002 and revised in July 2002, at the final session of the Preparatory Commission.[37]

This paper intended to reflect that progress made so far should hopefully serve as point of departure for debates to be continued in the Assembly of States Parties.

The document follows the methodological approach suggested during the final phase of the Preparatory Commission and therefore distinguishes between the concept of "crime of aggression" and "act of aggression". In light of the nature of the International Criminal Court intended to deal only with individual criminal responsibility and taking into account the wording of article 5 of the Statute as well as the mandate of the Preparatory Commission, the discussion paper focuses exclusively in the definition of the crime of aggression and deliberately refuses to enter into the definition of the act of aggression which entails State responsibility. By so doing, it abandons the lengthy controversy between the generic vs. list approach, which was very much linked to the contents of Resolution 3314.

In light of this approach, the discussion paper refers in paragraph 1 to the definition of the "crime of aggression" which is based on an updated formulation of the definition provided by the Nuremberg Charter and the jurisprudence of the International Tribunal. This definition encapsulates one of the few common understandings that transpired during the debates: the common assumption that only leaders of a State can be criminally held responsible of the crime of aggression:

> For the purpose of the present Statute, a person commits a "crime of aggression" when, being in a position effectively to exercise control over or to direct the political or military action of a State, that person intentionally and knowingly orders or participates actively in the planning, preparation, initiation or execution of an act of aggression which, by its character, gravity and scale, constitutes a flagrant violation of the Charter of the United Nations.

Immediately after this definition, the text includes three variations which refer to the issue of the threshold.[38] While one of the variations stipulates that no threshold is in fact required, the others include as thresholds two of the ideas put forward along the debates in order to narrow the uses of force that should be included under the definition of aggression:

---

[37] PCNICC/2002/2 Add.2 presented by the former coordinator, Mr. Tuvaku Manongi from Tanzania.

[38] See *supra* p. 170.

Paragraph 2 of the discussion paper relates the "act of aggression". The document is based on the premise that the definition of the act is not required since this concept relates to State responsibility and has already been defined by the international community through resolution 3314. Therefore, this part of the document simply refers to this resolution by stating that:

> For the purpose of paragraph 1, "act of aggression" means an act referred to in United Nations General Assembly resolution 3314 (XXIX) of 14 December 1974, which is determined to have been committed by the State concerned.

Paragraphs 4 and 5 and the multiple variations contained therein relate to the issue of conditions to exercise jurisdiction. This issue is probably far more difficult to resolve than the definition of the crime. The document does not even attempt to push a way forward among the multiple proposals and remedies proposed during the discussions. However, the discussion paper does move forward from the ambivalent views reflected in the content of article 5 of the Statute by accepting the assumption that the Security Council has the primary role in defining the act of aggression for the purpose of the crime. To this effect, paragraph 4 of the discussion paper states that:

> Where the Prosecutor intends to proceed with an investigation in respect of a crime of aggression, the Court shall first ascertain whether the Security Council has made a determination of an act of aggression committed by the State concerned. If no Security Council determination exists, the Court shall notify the Security Council of the situation before the Court so that the Security Council may take action as appropriate.

This assumption is of course without prejudice of alternative remedies to be provided, if any, in case of inaction by the Security Council. These alternative remedies include all ideas put forward during the debates. Therefore, it is proposed that in the case that the Security Council does not determine the existence of the act of aggression, there are three possible courses of action: 1) The Court can do the determination itself; 2) The Court cannot continue; 3) Another organ of the U.N. system determines the existence of the act of aggression, either the General Assembly or the International Court of Justice acting within its consultative jurisdiction.

Conclusions

It is to be hoped that the Assembly of States Parties will be able to make progress in respect to the definition of the crime of aggression and the conditions to exercise jurisdiction. Discussion during and after the Rome Conference demonstrate that there is no easy way out to the problems raised. It is quite clear by now that there will no quick "fix" to the issues involved, since it will be essential for any solution to be very widely accepted. This is a political must that has been transformed into a legal obligation by Article 5 of the Statute, which requires a provision on aggression to be adopted in accordance with Articles 121 and 123 of the Rome Statute. These articles provide for a cumbersome amendment process. An amendment would have to be voted in favor by a two-third majority of States Parties at a review conference to be convened seven years after the entry into force of the Statute. Taking into account this procedure it is clear that for a formulation to see the light, delegations will need to deploy all efforts to persuade and convince others of the benefits of their own formulations.

The conditions for exercise of jurisdiction over the crimes of aggression raise not only thorny political difficulties, but also technical problems that need to be addressed. From the latter perspective, it is important to understand that a predetermination of an act of aggression, by whatever organ, will have a tremendous impact on the criminal proceedings. The impact and the consequences for the ICC itself and for the rights of the accused need to be discussed further, in particular the defenses that that person could invoke in light of a predetermination of the act, and taking into account that the person would not only be linked to the State, but be considered, by definition, one of its leaders.

There is no justification to abandon, with respect to the crime of aggression, the stringent standards of legality that were applied to the definition of other crimes within the jurisdiction of the Court. The crime of aggression should not be treated differently than the crimes within the jurisdiction of the Court. Precisely because of the political nature of the issues involved, every effort should be made not to depart from the principle of legality, which should be perceived not only as a safeguard for the rights of the accused but as the best protection for the credibility of the Court as well.

Index